How To Succeed With People

Remarkably Easy Ways to Engage, Influence and Motivate Almost Anyone

Paul McGee

CAPSTONE

Illustrations (section title pages) © Fiona Osborne

Registered office
Capstone Publishing Ltd. (A Wiley Company), John Wiley and Sons Ltd, The Atrium, Southern Gate, Chichester, West Sussex, PO19 8SQ, United Kingdom

For details of our global editorial offices, for customer services and for information about how to apply for permission to reuse the copyright material in this book please see our website at www.wiley.com.

The right of the author to be identified as the author of this work has been asserted in accordance with the Copyright, Designs and Patents Act 1988

Reprinted May 2013, June 2013, August 2013, June 2014, April 2015, June 2015, March 2016

Wiley publishes in a variety of print and electronic formats and by print-on-demand. Some material included with standard print versions of this book may not be included in e-books or in print-on-demand. If this book refers to media such as a CD or DVD that is not included in the version you purchased, you may download this material at http://booksupport.wiley.com. For more information about Wiley products, visit www.wiley.com.

Designations used by companies to distinguish their products are often claimed as trademarks. All brand names and product names used in this book and on its cover are trade names, service marks, trademark or registered trademarks of their respective owners. The publisher and the book are not associated with any product or vendor mentioned in this book. None of the companies referenced within the book have endorsed the book.

Limit of Liability/Disclaimer of Warranty: While the publisher and author have used their best efforts in preparing this book, they make no representations or warranties with the respect to the accuracy or completeness of the contents of this book and specifically disclaim any implied warranties of merchantability or fitness for a particular purpose. It is sold on the understanding that the publisher is not engaged in rendering professional services and neither the publisher nor the author shall be liable for damages arising herefrom. If professional advice or other expert assistance is required, the services of a competent professional should be sought.

Library of Congress Cataloging-in-Publication Data
McGee, Paul, 1964–
   How to succeed with people : remarkably easy ways to engage, influence and motivate almost anyone / Paul McGee.
      1 online resource.
   Includes index.
   Description based on print version record and CIP data provided by publisher; resource not viewed.
   ISBN 978-0-85708-295-4 (ebk) – ISBN 978-0-85708-296-1 (cbk) – ISBN 978-0-85708-297-8 (ebk) – ISBN 978-0-85708-289-3 (pbk.)   1. Interpersonal communication.   2. Interpersonal relations.   3. Success.   I. Title.
   BF637.C45
      158.2–dc23
                                                    2013003564

A catalogue record for this book is available from the British Library.

Chapter title pages designed by Andy Prior Design
Cover design: Binary & The Brain

Set in 11/15 pt New Baskerville Std by Toppan Best-set Premedia Limited
Printed in Great Britain by TJ International Ltd, Padstow, Cornwall, UK

To the memory of Clive Gott
and Kenny Harris.

Miss you guys.

Contents

What's the big deal about this people Stuff?

I wonder if there may be some people you either live or work with who might be secretly or perhaps even publically scoffing at the fact that you're reading this book. Isn't all this stuff better off compartmentalized in the "pink and fluffy" box?

So do they have a point?

Absolutely.

Not.

Let me ask you a few questions.

- Do you know talented people who are currently disengaged and demotivated at work?

- How much does the success of your business depend on the quality of your relationships with customers and clients?

- Are there talented people who've left your organization and the main reason was due to their poor working relationship with their boss?

- Have there been relationships in your personal life that started off well but have now withered and died?

- Does the way you personally handle conflict tend to make things better or worse?

- Are there close family members who no longer speak to each other because of their inability to resolve a conflict?

- Do you know young people who can't wait to leave home because of their relationship with their parents?

- Has your education equipped you with a set of skills necessary to get the best out of yourself and your relationships with others?

Thought-provoking questions eh?

Now let me ask you some more.

So this is all pink and fluffy stuff, right?

It has no real impact on the quality of people's performance at work?

It has no impact on the bottom line?

It has no effect on the quality of your personal relationships?

Yeah right.

If people believe this is just pink and fluffy stuff, what are they?

A comedian?

Deluded?

Scared?

The fact is, if you're a woman reading this, the odds are you're probably already convinced of the importance of this book. However, some men (I'm glad to say not all) are still caught up in their antiquated and outdated machismo and need a wakeup call.

Some have already had one. Some have started to move with the times. Many more need to follow. And I write that as a fully paid up member of the male species.

However, whatever your gender, whatever your age, perhaps it's time to admit this:

Bite Size Wisdom

> The soft stuff is the serious stuff. It's a big deal

So let's quit playing games that "people are our biggest asset," and then spend hardly any time, energy or resources in equipping them to fulfil their potential. Let's kiss goodbye to tick box training and sign up to the fact that *we all* need help in knowing how to get the best out of ourselves and others. Especially in these challenging, uncertain and unpredictable times.

Let's ditch this pink and fluffy illusion once and for all and face facts.

Succeeding with people is a very big deal. And the ability to do so has perhaps never been as important as it is now.

Agree?

What does success mean to you?

Why not press pause for a moment and consider this question:

What does succeeding with people actually mean to you?

Do you hope more people will like you? Listen to you? Buy from you? Agree with you?

Is it a way for you to become more convincing and be more persuasive? Is it about you managing people more effectively or being a better parent? Or is the person you need to get on better with actually yourself?

You see, "success" means different things to different people.

None of us are starting from the same point, or with the same priorities.

So what does it mean for you? How will you know that reading this book has been worthwhile?

What do you want to do more of?

What do you want to do less of?

A lot of people read for pleasure. Fine. But wouldn't it also be worthwhile reading with purpose?

OK, well let's begin by setting the scene, so that you're clear on what you can and cannot expect from reading this book and why I've taken the approach I have in writing it.

Let's Set the
Scene

So you've decided to read a book about succeeding with people. Firstly, thanks for choosing this one. I hope you find reading it to be a valuable investment of your time and helpful on a number of different levels.

To begin with, let me explain why I've written the book and also why I've written it the way I have.

I guess unless you're a recluse or a monk who's taken a vow of silence whilst living in some isolated location, then interacting with people is part of day to day life. Despite our rapidly growing relationship with technology dealing with people in a visible or virtual sense is something few of us can escape.

But here's the deal.

None of us are magically born with a set of skills and insights to deal with the challenges of life and the people we encounter.

Seven billion people currently inhabit this planet, and by 2050 that figure is likely to be around 9 billion. That's a lot of people. Now I know you're not going to meet them all (no matter how big an extrovert you are), but the reality is the number of people you interact with in just a few months of your life is likely to exceed the number your great grandparents encountered in their entire lifetime.

Throw into the melting pot of those encounters with people economic uncertainty, globalization, information overload, twenty-four/seven living, increased expectations, the rise and role of the internet, cultural differences and you've got yourself quite a complex concoction.

The bottom line?

Our ancestors never lived in a world even remotely close to the one we're living in now. And whilst there may be an instruction manual for your iPad and your smartphone there isn't one specifically for dealing with people.

Here's the reality.

People are both predictable and unpredictable. Simple and complex. They can be kind. They can be killers. They give. They grab. They're compassionate. They're complacent. They're amazing. They're awful. They love. They hate. They're shaped by their past whilst living in the present.

So I'm not going to give you any bull here. I'm going to tell it as it is.

Faced with such a list of contrasting traits that people possess, the best we can hope for in dealing with them are some really helpful guidelines.

But no guarantees.

Now that's not to say there isn't some good news.

You see, despite the plethora of contradictions that make people who they are, there are some simple ideas, strategies and approaches that will help you build better relationships in both your personal and professional life. There are no magic wands, but they will significantly increase your chances of succeeding with people.

As a professional speaker and coach I've worked in 36 countries to date, across four continents. And here's one thing I've learnt: Although colour and creed may differ, whether I'm working in America, Africa, Australia, Asia or on my doorstep in Europe, what unites us is greater than what divides us.

In my experience we all have an insatiable drive to improve our lives – sometimes out of necessity, but often driven by our need for security and a sense of purpose.

Most of us want our children to have better lives than our own.

Many of us crave meaning and find it in religion, relationships or belonging to a particular cause or group.

Most of us intuitively know right from wrong.

But there are differences.

Culture, upbringing, age and religion help create those differences and shape our behaviour (I'm particularly fascinated by the way culture influences how we interpret other people's behaviour – for instance, avoiding eye contact in one culture is a sign of respect, but in another it has the opposite effect).

So I want at the outset to acknowledge those differences, and to reassure you I won't be providing a one-size-fits-all approach to dealing with people. However, I do want to raise your awareness and understanding of both yourself and others and provide insights and ideas you can use immediately. Both in and outside of work. Just be aware that you need to tailor them to your own particular situation, culture and current context.

Therefore make sure you use the ideas that are most relevant and realistic for you, recognizing what may work in one situation will fail in another. That's how life is and people are sometimes. So being flexible will be key.

Remember, no matter how good an idea is, it still needs to be used in the right way, in the right context, at the right time. After all . . .

Bite Size Wisdom

A fire extinguisher could be invaluable. But it's no use to a drowning man

Why is the book written the way it is?

There will always be lovers of books. For some people nothing can beat a good novel. But what percentage of the population enjoys wading through a business or self-help book? My guess is it's quite small.

How many people purchase business and self-help books but never finish them?

My guess is quite a lot.

So in an age when we seem cash rich but time poor and where we communicate via blogs and tweets and less through long books I wanted to achieve the best of both worlds.

A book that contains easy bite size wisdom that won't cause indigestion and can be read in bite size chunks.

A book that once consumed won't leave you bloated with information but rather energized and inspired with insights and ideas.

Oh and you'll notice something else.

What you're about to read is both simple and straightforward.

That's deliberate.

My goal is to help you become better at understanding, communicating and connecting with people.

It's not to massage your intellectual ego.

Steve Jobs spent his life trying to make the complex simple. Now I'm no Steve Jobs, but that's what you will find in this book.

Simplicity.

Straightforwardness.

A desire to cut to the chase.

Ideas and insights communicated in a bite size way.

You will also find honesty. I will share my mistakes and successes, and what I learnt from both.

And you will be challenged. There may be occasions when you're made to feel slightly uncomfortable.

You weren't expecting that, were you?

We like to feel good about ourselves. We like to feel we don't have to do a great deal to achieve success. If you're like me you'd quite like the very act of reading a book to magically transform you.

Beware of that trap. You see, we can delude ourselves into believing that the greater our knowledge the greater our success.

So let me be very straight with you.

I've been on this planet a long time. I've met some very knowledgeable failures. I've met some highly intelligent people who are highly incompetent with people.

Knowledge is a start but it's no guarantee of a successful finish. Neither is having a high IQ.

So along the way expect to be challenged not just to read the book but actually to do something with what you read. However, I promise I'll also include material that will raise the occasional smile. I really do hope you enjoy what you're reading, as well as find yourself being challenged by it at times.

You may also find some chapters more relevant than others. Succeeding with people is a big topic that covers a wide range of issues. Some topics covered are equally important both in and outside of work, but others do have more of a workplace bias.

Hopefully all the content is of interest, but some will be of real importance. So take hold of what is most applicable and perhaps share some of the other ideas with the people around you.

The first section gives you the opportunity to "Stop and Understand" people and to explore what can and can't realistically be achieved in your encounters with others. The second section helps you to "Move On" by using specific strategies to successfully deal with people in a variety of situations and contexts.

Finally, under no circumstances ever underestimate the power and impact of brief and simple ideas to help you on your journey to be successful with people.

But remember this: They're easy to do. They're also easy not to do.

The choice is yours.

Happy reading!

Paul McGee, 2013

Stop, Understand

People
can't be
fixed

Clare seemed very distressed. "I'm thirty years old, unemployed and still live at home with my parents. There are only two reasons why I can't get a job. Either there's something wrong with the world or there's something wrong with me. Clearly the world isn't to blame for where I'm at in life at present, so the problem clearly lies with me. I need fixing. Can you help?"

Wow. I'd only asked her how she was.

Clare had a very black and white view of life – perhaps more so than most of us. But she fell into a trap I believe many of us can fall into.

Believing people can be fixed.

Such people believe there must be a formula. A cure. Some instant solution that will remedy their problem, either with themselves or someone else.

Bite Size Wisdom

> Stop looking for quick fix solutions to complex, long-term problems

Well in case you hadn't noticed, people are not machines. A car or a computer may need a faulty part replacing before it's functioning again, but people are a little more complex. And as soon as you start looking to "fix" people or "fix" yourself you're in trouble.

The problem is we're so used to getting "things" fixed we start believing we can also do the same with people.

The reality is very different.

If you've got trouble with your phone you can ring a helpline and follow the step by step instructions on how to resolve it. Voila. Before you know it your problem is sorted. Carefully follow the instructions on how to erect your flat pack furniture and before your very eyes emerges your own TV stand with matching set of tables (although to be fair the ones I build end up looking more like a double wardrobe).

But there are no instruction manuals when it comes to dealing with people. Religions may lay out guidelines and principles to live by, but not step by step instructions. If there were such a manual it would have to be a very thick one.

Why?

We're complex. We're inconsistent. We react differently to the same event depending on our mood at that particular moment.

When we interact with others there can be a clash of cultures, egos and personalities.

The reality is you cannot treat everybody the same and expect the same outcome. Life, I'm afraid, is just not like that.

Bite Size Wisdom

Avoid the trap of taking a one-size-fits-all approach to dealing with people

So stop looking to fix people. Stop searching for that magical three point plan that is guaranteed to resolve all your issues. Plenty of writers and speakers promise such solutions.

I believe they're wrong.

Ideas, insights and principles are great.

Suggestions can be helpful.

Techniques may enhance your chances of success.

But let's not kid ourselves that results are guaranteed.

We're dealing with people.

Not motor cars or mobile devices.

So take time to explore lots of ideas in this book that will help you, but let's not fool ourselves that simple solutions exist for everyone's problem.

They don't.

And people cannot be fixed.

Helped? Absolutely.

Encouraged to see things differently? Possibly.

Motivated? Maybe.

Engaged? Perhaps.

Understood more than they currently are? Definitely.

The good news is we can significantly increase our chances of doing all of the above, but never forget this:

You can't control people. But you can do lots to influence them.

Oh and one other thing. They'll never be as straightforward as machines.

Ever.

Most people suffer from S.A.D.S.

E ver known anyone for years and then realized you know lots about them but they actually know very little about you? Ever asked anyone about their weekend but they've never thought to ask you about yours?

Ever worked with someone who seems to possess a similar set of social skills to Genghis Khan and who seems completely oblivious to the fact?

Ever met someone who continually finishes off your . . . sentences for you . . . often incorrectly?

Ever worked with someone who has an annoying habit of talking over people in team meetings and who you're convinced has never really listened to anyone but themselves in their entire life?

Ever met someone who seems very insightful about everyone but themselves?

You have?

Then you've probably met someone suffering from S.A.D.S. **S**elf **A**wareness **D**eficiency **S**yndrome. Of course the very nature of this condition (which I hasten to add is not an official medical term) means the person suffering from it is entirely unaware of the fact.

They're oblivious to their behaviour.

They have no realization of the impact their behaviour is having on others.

And guess what?

Their chances of actually reading a book like this and recognizing they might be a S.A.D.S. sufferer are only slightly above zero. And even if by some remote chance they did find themselves reading this book (presumably because their manager, friend or partner bought it for them) it's still highly unlikely they would recognize themselves in this section.

Which, ironically, is in itself one of the main symptoms of S.A.D.S.

And as you're reading this section you're probably thinking of people in your world who suffer from it, aren't you?

But before you sit back and relax into your armchair of smugness beware of the following.

You yourself may be prone to bouts of S.A.D.S.

To some degree at least.

Now before you start protesting at such an unfounded accusation, recognize that all of us have our blind spots.

Yes even you. And me. (And I'm the one who came up with the term!)

Now some people are definitely more self-aware than others.

The nature of certain jobs like counselling, teaching and nursing encourages people to self-reflect. And I recognize many other professions will do too.

In some organizations I've worked with, to encourage self-reflection and increase self-awareness managers not only give their staff feedback but the staff also give feedback to their managers. That isn't always a comfortable experience but it does help people to gain an insight into their behaviour and how they're perceived by others.

It's also not an exercise that's designed solely to point out people's faults but to provide a balanced perspective on how others see you, which will include highlighting many of your positive traits that you may take for granted.

And all of the above can help us be less prone to S.A.D.S. However, the following piece of wisdom is one to reflect on and chew over:

Bite Size Wisdom

Rarely do we truly see ourselves as others see us

Now like with many illnesses there's a spectrum in terms of the severity of S.A.D.S. In extreme cases there may even be a medical reason for people's seemingly gross lack of interpersonal skills and self-awareness such as some forms of autism (which in certain cases may be undiagnosed).

But all of us can from time to time suffer from S.A.D.S., even if only mildly.

Now you may believe you're more self-aware than most people you know, and even taking the time to reflect on the question "How self-aware am I?" would be a good indication of that fact. So too would be taking the time to read this book.

They're all positive signs, but they don't guarantee that you have high levels of self-awareness and that you truly understand yourself and your impact on others.

You may actually fall into the trap of devouring this kind of material and believe acquiring knowledge is the key to you succeeding with people.

It isn't.

It's what you do with what you know that counts.

Knowledge only takes you so far. It's when you decide to start doing something, or perhaps just as importantly stop doing something, that you begin to see the fruit of that knowledge.

So recognize that although you may encounter people who clearly are suffering from a strong case of S.A.D.S. we can all experience mild symptoms.

This insight will help you understand why some people you encounter will be very difficult to deal with but it will also keep you humble enough to recognize that none of us are immune from it and that we all need help to improve from where we are now.

Bite Size Challenge

1. When was the last time you asked someone close to you to give you their perspective on how you come across to them and others?

2. Ask six people in your life to come up with 10 words to describe you. Reflect on those words and see if there are any surprises or ones you wish weren't there. Then ask for more feedback on why they came up with those words, and any suggestions they might have to help you accentuate the positive aspects of your character and reduce the less positive ones. (Remember though, you're working with people's perceptions of you, which could be influenced by all kinds of factors. So look for common themes in the feedback you receive.)

Some
people
are
l**i**ghtbulbs

I trained to be a probation officer as part of my degree. People and how they behave fascinate me. But having studied for four years I decided not to pursue it as a career.

There were lots of reasons for my decision. But during interviews for other types of jobs I didn't want to get bogged down in explaining these reasons why. I had already fallen into that trap previously, where my interview focused more on the reasons why people commit crime and why I didn't feel cut out to work with such people rather than the job I was actually applying for.

So I implemented a cunning plan that dealt with the question as to why I didn't want to be a probation officer speedily and succinctly.

It went as follows:

Interviewer: So why didn't you want to pursue a career as a probation officer?

Me: Well to put a slight twist on an old joke, "How many probation officers does it take to change a lightbulb? One. But only if the lightbulb wants to change."

Now I suspect as you're reading the above you are not currently doubled up in laughter and wondering why I don't have my own comedy show. I'm wise enough to know that the world of comedy is not about to be turned upside down with my sudden appearance onto the scene.

But here's my point.

Whether it was due to stunned amazement that I had said something so unfunny or the fact they felt I had said something deeply profound and therefore didn't want to appear stupid, most interviewers smiled (well slightly) and moved onto their next question.

My cunning plan had worked.

Result.

And the reason for the above anecdote?

Well there are actually some people in life who are lightbulbs.

They do refuse to change.

And actually if you want to succeed with people then don't waste vast amounts of time and energy trying to change people who don't want to change.

By all means try. For a while.

But be careful.

Bite Size Wisdom

Don't delude yourself into thinking that you can automatically succeed where everyone else has failed

To put it bluntly, when it comes to dealing with some people, rearrange into a well-known phrase or saying:

"Brick wall banging like head your against a."

So why might someone behave like a lightbulb and not want to change?

Here are two reasons:

(i) They want to stand out from the crowd. They like to appear different from everyone else and always take the opposite viewpoint. This is not done for genuine reasons but because it meets their need for attention and sense of self-importance. They might actually enjoy winding others up. Do you know anyone like that? Well recognize that people behave in a way that gets their needs met.

Bite Size Wisdom

We all need to feel important – it's just that some people damage their relationships in their desire to achieve it

(ii) Some people have a very fixed view about the world and life in general. They know what they believe and what is right and what is wrong. And there can be a real sense of safety and security in this belief. It's comfortable. The last thing they want is for this to be challenged or for their world to be rocked.

So why be open to change? Why explore other possibilities? Why make myself feel uncomfortable?

Far safer to stand firm. Resist. Be cynical.

You see, it takes courage to change at times. It takes humility to admit you may be wrong. And some people are simply not courageous or humble enough to do so.

Harsh?

Perhaps. But it may well explain why some people remain lightbulbs.

Bite Size Wisdom

Remember, people's stubbornness is a choice. It's not a medical condition

But there is some good news. People don't have to remain a "lightbulb." They can change. But here's the key: Only if *they* want to. Remember, they'll do so for *their* reasons, not yours. And perhaps only if they're helped to do so.

It's possible that some people's "lightbulb" behaviour is only temporary. So meeting their need to feel important and providing plenty of support in times of change can help. So too can admitting your own struggle with change at times. So look out for ideas in the rest of this book that might help switch them on. You see, it's possible that you've been flicking the wrong switch so far. But what you're about to read might help you find the right one.

Bite Size Challenge

How fixed in your outlook would you say you are? How easy do you find it to change your mind or opinion about someone? Can you think of an example where you have changed your viewpoint about a person or situation?

Why Intelligent people do stupid things

E ver witnessed the behaviour of someone and thought "I can't believe they'd do something so stupid"?

Ever thought to yourself "I can't believe I just did that. What was I thinking?"

Ever wondered why some people fail to see the obvious answer to a problem when it's staring them right in the face?

I certainly have.

Part of my role in my business is to coach people. Often the coaching is related to how they can improve as a communicator and presenter, but sometimes the coaching is more focused on particular issues people are facing in their professional or personal lives.

Here's what's interesting.

When I'm emotionally detached from the situation I find my ability to see the cause of the problem and the possible solutions comes quickly and easily.

But there's a problem.

When I'm emotionally involved in the situation, when it's to do with my business, one of my team, one of my clients, or it's related to something in my personal life then my clarity becomes cloudy.

It's as if my glasses are permanently steamed up. I've been emotionally hijacked. My brain can become scrambled and what might be an obvious way forward to someone else can remain distant and elusive to me. A lack of sleep, often triggered because we're worrying about a situation, will further exacerbate our lack of rational thinking. Tiredness can trigger terrible decisions.

That's why seemingly rational, intelligent, successful people do stupid things. That's why rational, intelligent, successful people miss the obvious.

So when we're closely involved in a situation or physically and emotionally tired, our rational perspective often takes a back seat. And in its place steps up our emotional brain, which takes a firm grip of the controls of our decision making. Sometimes with dire consequences.

Bite Size Wisdom

Your emotions can cloud the view to your solutions

That's why at times it's absolutely critical that you *don't* strike whilst the iron is hot. Because when you do there's a strong chance that someone is going to get burnt. (You may just want to re-read that last point again. It could save you a lot of heartache in the future.)

Remember, when you're feeling either "mad," "bad" or "sad" you're not thinking straight. And often when we're in an emotional state we look for a short-term solution to a long-term problem. Our brains drive us to act not think.

So what does this look like in reality?

Parents can lash out with totally inappropriate and disproportionate punishments for their children. "You're grounded for three months."

Managers speak first and think later, "I never want him near this building again."

Customers can wildly overreact to a minor issue and go to extraordinary and time consuming lengths to argue their case.

If any of this seems familiar to you then welcome to dealing with the human race. It's not easy, is it?

So don't be deceived by our technological advances and our sophisticated ways of living. Deep down we still show remarkable similarities to our evolutionary ancestors.

Bite Size Wisdom

Our ways of communication may have evolved, but sometimes our ways of thinking haven't

So please, never ever assume that logic is running the show. It isn't.

And it's not just something other people are prone to. You're prone to this form of illogical and irrational thinking and behaviour as well. Drugs and alcohol will exacerbate our "stupidness," but so too will increased stress.

I'm really not exaggerating when I say *"stress makes you stupid."*

And conversely so too can feelings of high elation that can lead us into making rash promises and rash decisions whilst we're still caught up on an emotional high. Despite our later regrets our pride can kick in and make us feel compelled to stick with these promises and decisions. We can convince ourselves that to change our mind might appear foolish. Yet the reality is not changing your mind and admitting you may have acted rashly is stupid. But that's the danger when we allow our emotions to completely hijack our decisions.

Bite Size Wisdom

Never underestimate intelligent people's ability to make really stupid decisions

So as you read on look for ideas to manage your emotions more effectively and by doing so be more effective and less reactive in dealing with people.

Bite Size Challenge

If you've already overreacted to a situation or a person what will you do to ensure a better outcome next time?

You get what you tolerate

I remember years ago going on a two week residential management course for graduates. I was one of the chosen few to be selected for this apparently highly prestigious course. Over the two weeks we explored models (business ones that is), theories and philosophies of management. We did role plays, games and even spent time outside jumping off a 40 foot telegraph pole (with the aid of a safety harness of course).

At times it was fun.

At times I felt completely out of my depth.

And at times I wondered how on earth what I was learning about had anything to do with the real world. As I look back on the experience I remember only one thing. Jumping off that telegraph pole.

I certainly don't recall any advice or pearls of wisdom that have stood me in good stead since. I don't recall discovering anything new about myself, except that if you give me a set of business accounts to read I might as well be looking at an ancient long lost Hebrew manuscript.

I didn't feel equipped in any way, shape or form to advance my management career. It was so disappointing to spend two weeks on a course and to have so very little to show for it. In my opinion it was a complete waste of the company's money and my time.

I wonder if you've ever had a similar experience? I hope not.

Now let's fast forward a few years from then. Despite my previous experience I was still keen to invest in my development and decided to attend a one day seminar in the UK, run by an American company called CareerTrack. For a relatively small sum of money you could turn up for a day and explore topics such as "How to deliver exceptional customer service" and "How to discipline employees and correct performance problems." (Sexy title eh? Bet you wish you'd been to that one don't you?)

I, along with a hundred or so other business people, were sitting in a hotel conference room listening to some American guy enthusiastically telling us about his family and which part of the US he was from. I remember thinking that if things didn't improve at least I'd only wasted a day of my time, not two weeks.

And then it happened.

Almost casually the speaker Harry Chambers remarked, "You may want to write down this next bit. If you're managing people I think you'll probably find it useful."

Then Harry gave us two statements. It's nearly 20 years since I attended the event but I've never forgotten them. They've become engraved into my memory. I hope they become engraved in yours too. Because if they do I believe they will influence how you deal with people.

Ready for them?

OK. Here goes.

"We receive the performance (or behaviour) we are willing to tolerate."

and

"My silence, denial or avoidance gives approval to the situation."

Simple statements.

But very powerful.

No complex management theories to wrestle with or in depth questionnaires to fill in. In fact I guess it probably only took me a couple of minutes to write them down. And yet I've been pondering them ever since.

In hindsight I realize they're obvious statements really. But we don't always see the obvious do we? So let's unpack each statement a little and see how they relate to our day to day lives.

Let's start with the first one; "We receive the performance (or behaviour) we are willing to tolerate."

If you tolerate people being continually late without there ever being any consequences, guess what will continue to happen?

Tolerate someone continually putting you down and that behaviour will continue.

Tolerate people underperforming in your team and they'll see no reason to change.

Tolerate poor service and that's what you'll continue to receive.

Tolerate the behaviour of a loved one even though it hurts you and the cycle will continue.

Here's the deal. Plain and simple.

Bite Size Wisdom

You get what you tolerate.
Problems persist because
we get used to them

The question is, are you happy with what you're currently tolerating? Or do you just simply moan about it but continue to accept it?

Right, now onto that second statement: "My silence, denial or avoidance gives approval to the situation." Let's chew over that one for a moment.

In a nutshell, the reality is your non-actions still have an impact. Doing nothing is still doing something.

Challenging stuff eh?

Bite Size Wisdom

Your silence is still
saying something

So are you comfortable with the messages you're sending to others by saying and doing nothing? Are you relaxed about how others might see and treat you as a result?

If you are, fine.

That's your choice.

But please don't continue to moan, complain and resent someone (or some organization) if the only thing you're prepared to do is . . .

absolutely nothing.

Bite Size Wisdom

No matter how much you want them to be, people are not mind readers

People sometimes behave in a state of blissful ignorance, oblivious and unaware of the impact of their behaviour on you and others. And that's unlikely to change if you say and do nothing.

But please hear me right. I'm not suggesting people will immediately change if you do confront their behaviour (and as we'll see later, there are effective and less effective ways to go about this) but at least it's a start. At least the issue is out in the open. Things might get messy, but at least the boil has been lanced and there's an opportunity to deal with what was hidden beneath the surface. An added bonus is it can provide an outlet for the potential anger and resentment that was possibly building up within you.

When you stop tolerating and start talking you lay down the path towards a better and potentially more positive relationship. And by doing so you're more likely to succeed in dealing with people.

Bite Size Challenge

Is there someone's behaviour you've tolerated for too long? Are you prepared to live with the consequences or is it time to challenge them?

Humiliation
is for
amateurs

Three young managers accosted me at the end of one of my business presentations. They had a problem with one of their team called Barry. Apparently he was their most difficult and awkward employee. In their years of managing him they informed me they'd tried everything to turn around his performance and attitude. They hoped a brief explanation of their challenge with Barry would extract from me a pearl of wisdom or golden nugget that would immediately transform his performance overnight.

It's fair to say their expectations of me were hugely unrealistic, although not entirely uncommon. Some people seem to think that because I write books and speak at conferences this somehow transforms me into some mystical guru who is able to reveal ancient ideas and wisdom which until that point had remained hidden from mankind.

Sadly I'm not.

Which is a pity really, because in some ways I could get quite used to the idea.

However, armed with these false hopes and a problem employee my three managers put me firmly on the spot.

"So what do you think we should do with Barry then Paul?"

I tried to look guru-like and also buy some time, so I answered their question with a question.

"What's been your approach with Barry so far?"

"Well, we've tried the obvious."

"The obvious?" I enquired.

"Well yeah, we've tried humiliation."

Although struggling to quite comprehend what I'd just heard I somehow managed to mumble another question and maintain my guru-like persona.

"And how did that go down?"

"Well to be fair Paul, it just seemed to make Barry worse."

"Really, you don't say" I said, trying to contain my amazement at what was clearly an entirely inappropriate and ineffective approach.

But our conversation got me thinking. Why on earth would they think that humiliating someone was an obvious approach?

Maybe these three managers were only copying their role models. Perhaps a parent, teacher or even their own manager had tried this strategy with them previously. Maybe they'd witnessed humiliation being used as a tactic on others.

Whatever their reasons, let's be clear. When it comes to dealing with people, humiliation is the hallmark of a malevolent dictator, a sign of someone who has their own self-esteem issues or an indication of a complete lack of knowledge and experience in dealing with others.

Bite Size Wisdom

Humiliating someone is not an indication of your strength. It's a reflection of your weakness

It's like crushing a nut with a chieftain tank. Unhelpful, unnecessary and wholly destructive.

It's the same with people. Deliberately humiliating someone is not a form of motivation, but it is laying down the foundation for bitterness, resentment and perhaps even revenge in the future.

In December 2008 the then manager of Hull City found his team 4–0 down to Manchester City in an English Premiership game. So, angered by his team's first half performance, the manager Phil Brown decided to conduct his half-time team talk on the pitch in front of the travelling Hull City fans. Players subsequently described being lectured by their manager in front of their own fans as a humiliating experience.

Up until that game, Hull City's record was Played 18 Won 7 Drew 5 Lost 6 – a total of 26 points. In their next 20 matches Hull City went on to win only 1 more game, losing 14 and drawing 5. That's just 8 points.

They survived relegation by a single point.

Some people do feel humiliated by their own performance, or because of a mistake they've made. In these cases and in this specific context it can make them determined to never face such an experience again. But this form of humiliation is self-inflicted. It's not the same as being humiliated by someone else.

Now if you do have to give someone some challenging feedback, please remember this: Where you say it and who's present when you say it can be just as important as the actual words you use.

Having worked in the Far East I'm aware of the importance in the Asian culture of "saving face." In other words, do all you can to ensure another person retains their self-respect, especially in front of others.

But let's not dismiss this as not being an important factor in Western culture also.

Here's the reality.

No one likes to look stupid, no matter what country they live in. A fundamental human need is a desire to feel competent, useful and valued.

So if you want to influence and engage people and switch them on to your way of thinking, then take humiliation for a hike.

Bite Size Wisdom

Only clowns are happy to look stupid

If you have something to say that is potentially negative or critical, consider the following points:

- Will I still want to say this in 24 hours?

- What's my end goal in saying what I'm about to say?

- Am I aware of the long-term effect my words may have on this person?

- Where am I best saying what I have to say?

- Who else, if anyone, needs to be there when I say it?

Some people are more naturally resilient than others. Perhaps they have thicker skin and can quickly brush off criticism. It washes over them. But humiliation is more than criticism. It strikes at the heart of a person's self-esteem. It wounds their pride. It attacks the core of their identity.

Being humiliated could literally crush some people psychologically, particularly if they're already demoralized and less thick skinned. And if the person on the receiving end of the humiliation is a child and the perpetrator is a parent the damage can be long lasting.

So make sure you check out the chapter "How to make criticism count, not crucify," and challenge your own motives behind what you're saying. Be honest, is it to help or hurt the other person?

To make sure your communication is seen as less of a personal attack, and in order to soften the blow, if you have something to say try a couple of the following ideas.

Firstly, when you disagree with someone you could ask "Do you mind if I play devil's advocate for a moment?" That way it's as if you've introduced another character into the conversation. You're actually gaining the other person's permission to challenge their ideas, not by doing so as yourself, but in your role as devil's advocate. It becomes far easier to challenge someone when you're "playing" this role and it de-personalizes what you're saying.

Secondly, remember people find it easier (not easy, but easier) and less painful to hear negative news from their mouth than from someone else's. So rather than telling people directly what you thought simply ask:

"What've you learned from that experience?"

followed by

"If you had a chance to do that again, what would you do differently?"

Now if they say "nothing" then you've got a bigger problem than you realized. Not only is this person incompetent, they're also oblivious to the fact! (And probably suffering from S.A.D.S. – see the chapter "Most people suffer from S.A.D.S.") To be honest this is rare, and asking such questions gives the other person time to reflect and hopefully come up with their learning and a better approach next time. As they've now started going down this track it also makes it easier for you to build on their thoughts and ideas and offer some of your own. This will feel to the other person like they're in a conversation with you rather than being criticized by you.

Finally another strategy that I've found hugely helpful in addressing a challenging and perhaps awkward situation whilst allowing the other person to save face is to ask them this question:

"If you were me what would you do?"

This again gives someone the opportunity to come up with their own ideas for a way forward and although you might not necessarily agree with them entirely, they're being treated more like an adult rather than a naughty child.

Make sure you take the above seriously. From children through to colleagues, the pain of being humiliated can have long-term negative consequences not just for them, but for you also. People may need to be challenged. They may need a wake-up call. But they do not need to be humiliated. Ever.

Bite Size Challenge

Which of these three strategies, "playing devil's advocate," asking "what've you learned and what would you do differently?" and "if you were me what would you do?" will you use to help rather than potentially humiliate someone?

Being **nice** won't always **work**

There's a huge myth around dealing with people that states you should always be nice to them. Whilst I'm not advocating you be nasty I am suggesting that one of the reasons you could be failing with people is because you're actually too nice.

Let me explain.

I was talking to a woman who was bemoaning her new female boss's recent arrival at the store where she worked. Morale had plummeted and I immediately leapt to the conclusion that this was due to the manager's inability to motivate and deal with her staff.

I was wrong. Well, to a degree anyway.

The staff were demotivated, but not for the reasons you would expect.

Their new boss was a great one for professional standards. She questioned why people were late getting to work or late back from breaks. She expected hard work from her employees and held regular team meetings.

This came as quite a shock in comparison with the previous manager's style of management, which at best could be described as "laid back and easy going."

Staff were not happy. Some had been used to ringing in sick on a Saturday morning after a heavy night out on Friday. Whilst the previous manager accepted they "had a bit of a cold" and told them not to worry, their new boss was less accommodating. Whilst not accusing them of lying, she seemed low on sympathy and high on making them aware of the consequences their absence was having on the rest of the team. Apparently things were now so bad some staff were contemplating leaving as they sought an easier ride somewhere else.

Their previous manager may well have been described as "nice." They were certainly popular. But the store was underperforming. The staff were exploiting the manager's relaxed and non-confrontational style.

Bite Size Wisdom

If your main goal in life is to be popular, audition to play the role of Snow White at Disney World

Here's the deal.

If you want to make a positive difference in life you need to recognize that means you're not always going to be liked by everyone. At times, just like the manager in the above example, you will be disliked. And that's OK. As the author Robin Sharma says:

Bite Size Wisdom

People with a need to be liked don't change the world

Powerful stuff eh?

Being too nice can also send mixed and unclear messages to others.

Let me explain.

Sometimes when nice people are pushed to a point where even they need to say something about someone's behaviour their message can still be lost in a sea of "diplomatic let's not cause offence waffle." Here's what I mean. I'll exaggerate the point to make the point:

"Hi, sorry to be a pain. I just wondered if at some stage when it's convenient, if it's not too much trouble, would it be OK if, and there's no rush, but would it be possible, when it works for you, if you wouldn't mind taking your foot off my neck. Thanks. I really do appreciate it."

The reality is people can exploit your niceness as a weakness. You're not succeeding with people with this approach.

You're failing.

OK there may be some perceived superficial benefits with such an approach. People may speak well of you. You may be popular. Even well liked. But are you succeeding? Really?

Bite Size Wisdom

To be successful with people it's more important to be respected than to be liked.

You may of course have built up such a good relationship with people that you're respected and liked. Great. Wonderful. But if I had to choose which is the most important of the two if I want to achieve success in life (apart from playing Snow White at Disney World) it would have to be respect.

Now please don't go out of your way to be nasty. But if an underperforming team member sees you as less of a soft touch and that challenging neighbour or awkward friend has decided to back down a little then perhaps you're discovering the benefits of not being too nice. You don't have to ditch your diplomacy to do so, but you do need to ditch the need to always be liked.

Bite Size Challenge

Has your niceness ever been exploited by others? Have you learnt from the experience? Is there a situation now where your "niceness" is actually damaging the relationship?

It takes
two to
tango

As a professional speaker I'm sometimes asked if I ever embellish a story, perhaps making it a little more interesting and amusing than it was in reality. And my honest answer?

Yes I do.

I see my role when speaking as not just to inform and inspire but also to entertain, and so for that reason I have on occasions exaggerated a particular point. (However, I think it's fair to say that most people don't really believe that the person who trained me in my first job was 6'3", had a shaven head along with the hairiest arms I'd ever seen . . . and was called Jackie.)

There are also occasions when for the sake of time and relevance I miss out certain details of a story. My goal is not to communicate 100% of the facts and give my audience too much detail but to get over a particular point. As to the question of whether I put a certain degree of spin on what I'm saying, I plead guilty as charged.

So why am I making this point?

Because I don't think such a practice is confined solely to my work. I can equally take the same approach when conversing socially. In fact, whatever the context I think all of us will at times put our own spin on things.

Perhaps more regularly than we realize.

This can especially be the case when we're talking to someone about a problem or disagreement we've had with another person.

Bite Size Wisdom

> Whenever we tell our version of events we instantly become our own personal spin doctor

Very often when we begin to recount a particular event or incident we'll have a tendency to immediately tell it with a certain degree of bias and emphasis. We might not even be aware we're doing it, but invariably we are. And to be fair it's unlikely that we'll want to present ourselves in the worst possible light. As a consequence, when we're telling our version of events certain information may be completely left out and the context or background to the event entirely overlooked.

So it's helpful to understand that we can *all* be prone to putting our own particular angle on a story and have a tendency to subtly alter and distort the facts in our favour. Sometimes without realizing we're doing so.

That's why when it comes to succeeding with people we need to be especially aware of our own personal in-built bias to do this. So remind yourself that on occasions (I recognize not all) it does take two to tango.

In other words, despite me being able to convince myself that the entire blame for a conflict or disagreement lies with another person, I need to challenge myself to take a look at what role I may have also played in contributing to the situation. I'm not suggesting there's equal blame or responsibility to be apportioned. Just recognize that you may, perhaps unintentionally, have also added to the conflict.

How?

Well there could be a number of reasons.

You may have made some wrong assumptions. Your intentions may not have been clear to the other person. Perhaps you had previously said or done something which had upset them. This list could go on and on.

But here's the challenge.

Our own contribution to the conflict can be hard to see when we keep re-telling the story with our own particular spin on it. Through the continual repeating of a story we can begin to believe our version of events is a complete and accurate representation of all the facts.

Trust me, it never is.

Bite Size Wisdom

Remember, life is rarely ever clear cut, black and white, right and wrong

It's complex, confusing, messy and grey at times. And it's within that context we play out our relationships with others.

Be careful, because we can be prone at times to quickly play judge and jury in a situation and condemn people immediately as a result. However, that's like listening to the facts of a crime from the prosecution's perspective and drawing a conclusion without listening to the case for the defence.

So tread with caution, because conflicts can escalate as a result of this blinkered approach. And an unwillingness to look at your own role in contributing to a particular misunderstanding or conflict can make a positive outcome harder to achieve.

The Gospel of Matthew puts it in a more challenging way than I do:

"Why do you look at the speck of sawdust in your brother's eye and pay no attention to the plank in your own eye?" (Matthew 7: 3, New International Version.)

Rather blunt I realize, but certainly worth reflecting on. Agree?

Bite Size Challenge

When was the last time you took a step back and asked "In what way is my behaviour contributing to this problem?"

No investment no return

I heard recently that a branch of a poorly performing retail store had been turned around by the introduction of a new manager.

That's not the most surprising thing you'll ever read is it?

But the next bit might be.

The hundred or so full and part time staff of the store reported one of the main reasons for their improved performance and increased morale was this:

The new manager used and remembered everyone's name.

They actually showed an interest in them as people, not just in their performance.

Now I'm sure there were many other things the new manager did to improve the performance of the store, but this seems to be the one that created the biggest impact on staff.

Not a pay rise. But remembering and using people's name.

Bite Size Wisdom

Never underestimate
the large impact of a
small gesture

In our never-stand-still, frenetic, multi-optional communication channel-filled world, it's easy to forget the following:

The power and importance of investing time in a quiet, uninterrupted face to face conversation with someone.

You see the reality is that it's easy to see people every day and yet not really know them.

It's easy to allow significant relationships to simply drift along on auto-pilot rather than be lived out intentionally.

It's easy to allow what was a good, vibrant healthy relationship to fade and ultimately fizzle out.

Not deliberately.

Not maliciously.

But simply through neglect.

You stopped making the time to talk.

To listen.

To question.

To laugh.

To do things together.

As a team. As a couple. As a family.

And the reasons?

Perhaps you were busy. Perhaps they were. Maybe there were so many other distractions. Maybe because there seemed no real need to catch up properly. Everything seemed fine. There were no big issues to address.

"Hey, if it ain't broke, don't fix it" may be the attitude adopted by some. However, that's not quite the approach you would take with a car, is it? Even if it's running smoothly you still take it for a service. It makes good sense to do so. It's an opportunity to replace or repair parts *before* they cause any damage. Making such an investment not only prevents problems occurring in the future, it also lengthens the reliability and life of the car.

Common sense really.

Maybe we need to take such an approach with our relationships. Long-term customers may appreciate a visit, staff may value the opportunity to both give and receive feedback. Loved ones may enjoy doing some simple things together like going for a walk or having a relaxed uninterrupted conversation that gives them the opportunity to re-connect emotionally.

Here's the deal:

Bite Size Wisdom

Great relationships with customers, colleagues or loved ones don't just happen magically. They take time.

Consciously or unconsciously there are factors that contribute to the success of a relationship both in and outside of work. And when you fail to invest any time with people, don't be surprised when you fail to see any return. The harsh truth is being too comfortable and too complacent can kill a relationship. Being too busy and distracted can lead to a breakdown between people in both a professional and personal setting.

Never assume the honeymoon period will last.

It won't.

Trust me.

I've learnt that from experience.

The nature of my work means I can be away from home on a regular basis. I can easily go days and on occasions weeks without seeing my wife and children. When I come home after all my travelling I really appreciate a little bit of quiet downtime and readjustment.

The problem is that if I'm not careful this can become a habit. My downtime by myself can become normality. It can become the rule, not the exception.

So I have to make some choices. Conscious choices.

So family meals are rarely if ever in front of the television, they're around our kitchen table. Time out with each other is diarized, not simply desired if we have time to squeeze it in.

With my son this has been easy to do. Our mutual love of football (if you can describe watching Bradford City and Wigan Athletic as football) determines that we'll often spend time together. Working with my wife also gives us the freedom and flexibility to take some time out with each other. And my mum has her weekly Wednesday night ritual when she comes round for dinner and lavishes the family with chocolate whilst reminding us to be careful with our weight.

However, with my teenage daughter Ruth it's been different. We share few common interests. I gave up my love of makeup, handbags and high heels a long time ago. But I became aware by the time she reached her tenth birthday that the main focus of our conversation had by then invariably begun to revolve around the state of her bedroom (which to be fair did resemble the aftermath of a tsunami and earthquake combined). We were drifting apart. I needed to make some changes.

The length of time I spend away from home has continued. But what I now do when I am home has changed. Unlike previously I no longer complain about being Ruth's taxi service. I now see that time in the car together as an opportunity for some natural, unforced conversation. We have the occasional meal out – just the two of us. She still spends some of that time texting mates – she's now a teenager after all – but we do have some time to be together. She seems to appreciate that. I wouldn't say we're best mates all of the time, but neither are we strangers. Once a year we even have a weekend together in London. I spoil her and in return she chooses clothes for me that make me look at least one step removed from middle-aged meltdown.

Her bedroom is still untidy.

I fail to comprehend her taste in certain types of music. Going to concerts in order to be bashed around in a mosh pit is still alien to me.

And I'll probably pass on the tattoos and body piercing. For the time being, anyway.

But I think we've laid down some solid foundations in terms of our relationship.

I hope that when she's older the investment we've made in her teenage years will stand us in good stead. We've certainly created some good memories and although I doubt her bedroom will ever be how I'd like it, I think our relationship with each other could be.

Of course, I'm aware you might not have a son or daughter. However, whether you have or haven't is not the issue, because the principle remains the same with customers, colleagues and loved ones. No investment, no return.

If you really believe people are important (and my guess is you do, or else you wouldn't have read this far) then quit hoping to *find* the time to invest in those relationships. *Make* the time. And this next point is crucial. Remember, investing doesn't necessarily mean talking. Sometimes the most important thing can be simply doing things together and sharing the experience.

And if you're a manager remember investing in people will also mean investing in their development. Recruiting talent can be a costly and time consuming exercise. But if you want to retain people recognize that you will need to invest in them if you want to see a return on their talent. Some managers say "What if we train people and they leave?" Well think about this:

What if you don't train people and they stay?

So invest some time with people, but also look for ways to invest in their development as well. (Hey, you might even want to pass this book to them.)

Bite Size Challenge

Who in your world requires more of your time and attention right now? Choose someone not out of guilt but genuine desire to build a better relationship and diary some time together. Why not do that now rather than reading any further? Go on then.

Section Two

Move On

Have realistic expectations

A few years ago I took part on the quiz show *The Weakest Link*, presented by the formidable TV host Anne Robinson.

I was 40 at the time and challenged myself to do something during the year that was a little bit different to mark what many people regard as a significant age. Appearing on the show was one of those things.

My goal perhaps surprisingly was not to win the show; quizzes and me go together about as well as fried fish and rice pudding, but rather to get the phrase SUMO – "Shut Up, Move On" mentioned at least a couple of times.

In terms of my goal I was very successful. "SUMO" was mentioned seven times, including by one of the other contestants and Anne Robinson herself. Result.

However, answering the questions correctly proved to be more challenging. To my surprise I did make a good start and was the "Strongest link" on one of the earlier rounds. But my success was short-lived and it wasn't long before I was vying with another contestant for a place back in the green room. We'd both received the same number of votes for who should be the weakest link, so the decision as to which of us went lay with the person who had been the strongest link that round. That happened to be a woman who it's fair to say I hadn't particularly clicked with during our time meeting up before the show. She generated the same amount of warmth towards me as a giant ice cube.

I sensed I was doomed.

I wasn't disappointed.

The woman who'd pronounced sentence on me and thus triggered my walk of shame was then questioned as to why she'd voted me off. I wondered if it was related to my ridiculously stupid answer to a relatively simple question. Or was it due to the fact that she thought my ignorance was faked and was part of a cunning ploy and that I could actually be a potential threat in the later rounds?

No.

So what was her reason?

You'll never guess.

She'd once read a book on motivation and it didn't work for her, and knowing a little of my background she believed I deserved to go.

That was it.

End of story.

Anne Robinson took great pleasure in telling me it was time to shut up and move on as I was now the weakest link. (If you'd like to see a brief clip of this please go to http://www.thesumoguy.com/videos/introducing-paul-mcgee.mp4. My appearance on the show is towards the end of this short video.)

As I reflected on my arch enemy's reason for voting me off it caused me to wonder if in many ways her attitude sums up the attitudes of many people in regards to themselves, other people and perhaps life in general – "I tried it once and it didn't work." Yet no one really thinks they can get fit by going to the gym once. Or lose a certain amount of weight because they gave up burger and fries for a day. And yet in other areas of life we do seem to hold on to unrealistic and unreasonable expectations.

Perhaps at the root of some of our disappointments, frustrations and conflicts are the unrealistic expectations we have of other people and how they should respond and behave in situations.

At times we may even seek to justify these feelings by saying "I would never behave like that if I was them."

But that's the point.

You're not them.

You won't always know their history, their background, their values or who their own role models have been. You don't necessarily know what current challenges and concerns they may be facing, or insecurities they're struggling with.

In his book *Confessions of a Conjuror* (Transworld Publishers, 2010) Derren Brown puts it this way:

"Each of us is leading a difficult life, and when we meet people we are seeing only a tiny part of the thinnest veneer of their complex, troubled existence."

OK, perhaps Derren is laying it on a little thick there, but I believe his words are worth reflecting on. Perhaps a little compassion and understanding on our part may be required at times.

Bite Size Wisdom

It's understandable that you want others to live up to your standards. But it's not always realistic

In relation to my "Weakest Link" opponent why would anyone think reading a book about motivation would magically transform them?

But they do.

Why would someone feel a complete lack of guilt about not giving their best at work?

But they do.

Why would someone make all kinds of promises to you without having the faintest intentions of actually delivering on them?

But they do.

Why do small children decide to have tantrums at the most inconvenient of times?

But they do.

So is this a call to lower your standards and raise a flag of surrender and passively accept whatever behaviour other people would care to throw in your direction?

No.

That's why this next point is crucial. Make sure you digest it.

Bite Size Wisdom

"Realistic expectations" does not mean low expectations

I do believe that a lot of the time your expectations will be met; but let's not be so surprised when on occasions they're not. And if you can develop this "realistic mindset" when dealing with others you will become less frustrated and disappointed in people.

However, make sure that if your expectations are not met you ask yourself if that's due to them being unrealistically high or because you haven't actually clearly spelt out your expectations to others?

You see I would love people to be as enthused as I am about personal development.

I would love everyone who hears me speak to be inspired, empowered and entertained.

But they're not.

In some cases (not too many, fortunately) it's the complete opposite.

Some people take an instant dislike to me and my material. If I could walk on water I'm convinced some people would turn round and say "that guy can't swim."

Reality rules.

And just as you can't please all of the people all of the time, similarly you won't be pleased by everyone all of the time.

It goes with the territory.

It's called life.

It's the reality of dealing with this amazing yet sometimes confusing and complex creature known as "homosapien."

To an extent we're all weird, wacky and wonderful, although in what proportion varies from person to person. (You may know a few people who score particularly high on weird and wacky. My kids certainly think I do.)

However, the above doesn't mean we should automatically expect the worst from others. Let me stress it's good to have high expectations of yourself and other people and to strive for excellence. But don't make them unrealistically high.

Let's recognize and sometimes even embrace our flaws and the flaws of others. As a general principle let's be more accepting rather than judgemental of others.

Bite Size Wisdom

Be more philosophical about people's behaviour, rather than emotional

However, don't compromise too much. Let's not be accepting of what is clearly unacceptable. Let's not abandon our standards, but be aware that it's not always realistic for everyone to meet them all of the time; especially from people who don't benefit from our age and experience.

Accept that there will be times when others will disappoint you. There will be times when others behave in a way very different to how you would. And when that happens, as I assure you it will, let's avoid making it into an unnecessary crisis or mini drama that causes us undue stress and anxiety and instead recognize sometimes you just need to SUMO: Shut Up, Move On.

Bite Size Challenge

Think of people who you feel have not met your expectations. Is that due to your expectations being unrealistic or because you didn't clearly communicate them?

Y̶ou may remember that in the earlier chapter "You get what you tolerate" we explored the challenges of tolerating and accepting other people's behaviour. This chapter is about the fact that on occasions it might be best to accept a situation or behaviour for the benefit of the long-term relationship.

Some may see this as contradictory advice.

It isn't.

As I mentioned earlier, if you want to succeed with people you need to avoid a one-size-fits-all approach. Being flexible and adaptable is crucial to dealing with people, so sometimes a different approach or strategy is required. Remember, a fire extinguisher is very useful – but not if you're drowning. That's why on occasions we really do need to let sleeping dogs lie.

But what "things" might you want to tolerate?

That's for you to decide. But here are a few questions that might help you make your decision.

1. What are the consequences of not tackling this issue? Am I happy and comfortable living with those consequences?

2. On a scale of 1–10 where 10 is extremely important, where would you rate your issue?

3. If you don't tackle the issue how important will it be in 6 months' time?

4. By leaving things as they are what message, if any, are you sending to others?

5. How strong a possibility is it that things will get worse if you say or do nothing?

6. Is it worth your time and energy addressing this issue in order to achieve what you want to achieve?

It's worth reflecting on this piece of wisdom:

Bite Size Wisdom

> Assertive people sometimes choose to be non-assertive

Perhaps the most important question to answer honestly in your own mind is: "By letting sleeping dogs lie am I comfortable both with the consequences of my decision and my reasons behind it?"

Please don't use this idea as a way to justify a weakness on your part. This is not an excuse to avoid confrontation. It's not meant to be your starting point in all relationship issues, but a possible strategy you might use in order to ensure the long-term success of a relationship.

Bite Size Challenge

Has a previous decision you've made not to address an issue been a conscious choice on your part or because you lacked a little courage and didn't want to be seen as unpopular?

There are times when I reflect on my interactions with others and I think I made a mountain out of a molehill over some things. And there are some relationships which have never been the same because I decided to tackle an issue.

That's unfortunate, but it is reality.

Perhaps it says more about the way I went about raising the problem than the actual problem itself (something we'll explore later in the book).

Equally there are a number of relationships where I've kept my counsel, decided to bite my lip and which I'm so glad I did.

You see, not everything is worth fighting for.

Being totally transparent about your feelings in all situations is not always necessary. Choosing to lose the occasional battle in order to win the overall war can be an effective strategy. Whilst choosing to be assertive all the time over every single issue is both tiring and boring. It can lead to issues escalating when they didn't need to, feelings being hurt and relationships being damaged.

Bite Size Wisdom

You don't always have to speak your mind. It's OK to shut up sometimes

Perhaps there may be an issue you're facing and it's best to let the scab heal on its own rather than continually picking at it.

Ultimately it's your call. Just remember, you do have choices.

Bite Size Challenge

Identify a current situation where you recognize it is probably better to let sleeping dogs lie.

Check out your attitude

I don't know if you've ever changed car, moved house or been pregnant (or known someone close to you who is). But if you have then you'll probably be aware of a strange phenomenon. Psychologists call it "attention awareness."

Let me explain.

When I was thinking of buying another car I suddenly started spotting that particular type of car everywhere. When I put my house up for sale, I then couldn't drive down a road without noticing "For Sale" signs. Neither could I read a newspaper without stumbling across an article about houses. And when my wife was pregnant in the 1990s (not the whole decade I hasten to add – just two nine month periods) she remarked on just how many women seemed to be pregnant at the moment.

Bite Size Wisdom

Your brain is very skilled in helping you find what you're looking for

As humans we're very adept at noticing what is relevant or important to us at that particular time.

OK. Big deal, you might be thinking. So why is that fact important to you and me? Well let's apply this same principle to how we are with people.

If you notice and talk about a particular positive or negative trait in another person you'll then continue to notice it (like I did with cars and houses, and my wife did with pregnant women). Once a habit or type of behaviour appears on your radar it's actually very difficult not to notice it in the future.

Consequently, if we're not careful we can actually develop a distorted picture of someone by either always noticing the positives, sometimes referred to as "the halo effect," or equally always noticing the negatives, which is referred to as "the horns effect." (The reason for horns is in connection with how the concept of the devil is often visually portrayed as having two horns.)

Now if you're struggling in a relationship with someone there's an extremely high chance that you will tend to notice and talk about their negative behaviours.

That's understandable. But remember this:

What you focus on magnifies.

And so begins a cycle. Your negative attitude towards someone is fuelled by you noticing negative things about them which in turn reinforces your negative views of them:

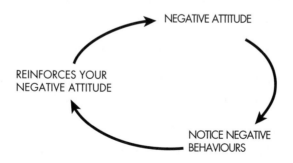

NEGATIVE ATTITUDE

REINFORCES YOUR
NEGATIVE ATTITUDE

NOTICE NEGATIVE
BEHAVIOURS

Bite Size Wisdom

In many ways your view
of people becomes a
self-fulfilling prophecy

Not only that, but if you're not looking for the positives in people you won't notice them.

So why's that the case?

It's all to do with how your brain works.

Aware of just how much information your mind is being bombarded with, the brain's attempt to help us avoid a mental meltdown is in many ways similar to an email spam filter. It filters out information that is not considered life threatening, relevant or highly unusual. And that all goes in the junk box.

And your attitude determines what goes in the junk box unopened.

So if you're *not* looking for the positives in people and only looking for the negatives, guess what ends up in the junk box?

Their positive traits and behaviours.

Meanwhile your inbox is filling up with examples of their negative behaviour.

So what's this insight got to do with your relationships with others? How will it help you to succeed with people? Well think of a person you don't get on with as well as you would like. Here are some questions to reflect on.

- What is it about their behaviour you don't particularly like?

- Is it possible you only notice their negative behaviour and fail to notice any of their more positive traits?

- What are the consequences of having a negative attitude towards them?

- If you had to acknowledge three positive traits about the person what would they be?

I'm not suggesting reflecting on these questions has now filled you with warm fuzzy feelings towards this other person. However, it might have led you to opening your junk mail and realizing there are some positive things about them that you may not have noticed before.

OK, now let me share with you an important and painful lesson from my own experience which illustrates the dangers of having a fixed negative view of someone and how your attitude affects your behaviour. As you're about to see, my experience would have been very different if I'd only thought about the previous questions.

Several years ago I was working with a company who were set up to support organizations who were making people redundant. I was hired to offer advice and support to staff who were losing their jobs.

Over time I got to know some people particularly well as I helped them compile CVs and coached them on interview techniques. Some of those people are now a distant memory, but there was one guy I'll never forget.

Mark.

He was a challenge.

The best way to describe him was that he was like a leech. He seemed to latch on to me and drain me of my life, my energy and my reasons for living. Five minutes with Mark felt like five hours with someone else.

It's fair to say he didn't exactly light up my life when he walked into my office.

Quite the opposite in fact.

It became quite a joke amongst other members of the team. Comments such as "I see your friend's in to see you later" were commonplace. And despite all my efforts to help Mark he remained unsuccessful in finding work. So he visited our offices even more.

Then I got some great news.

Mark had set himself up in business. Finally he would be off my books. Finally I would look at my appointment book without the sense of dread I had felt previously. Life felt good all of a sudden.

In a fit of overwhelming generosity I bought the three admin staff a small chocolate bar.

Each.

I returned to my own office with a sense of renewed optimism about life. In fact, if you'd asked me at that point could the England football team win a match on penalties at a major football tournament I would have probably answered "yes."

That's how good and optimistic I felt.

And then within moments my joyous world evaporated before me. As I looked out across the car park from my office window I saw a large white van pull up.

And Mark got out.

He walked towards our office.

I dashed back into reception to confront Vera the receptionist.

She had finished her chocolate bar.

"Vera, Vera," I squeaked, in a slightly startled "this isn't really happening to me" kind of voice.

"I've just seen Mark. He's heading here right now."

"Didn't you know?" Vera enquired in a rather casual, nonplussed way.

"Didn't I know what?" I replied, already beginning to regret my decision to buy those bars of chocolate.

"Well as part of our on-going service to Mark, he's going to be using our office as his office. He'll be using our stamps, our stationery, our photocopier. In fact, we should be seeing a lot more of him."

I was dumbstruck.

For once.

My brain struggled to process what Vera was telling me. And then in the darkness of my confusion there came a brief shaft of light.

Hide.

If I hid in the gents' toilets, Vera could tell Mark I'd gone out for lunch and he'd have to see one of my colleagues instead.

Not I confess an idea I'm particularly proud of in hindsight, but it seemed like a good one at the time.

However, I had no time to implement it. Before I knew it Mark was stood next to me.

"Alright Paul. How you doing?"

Despite my face portraying a deep sense of doom and gloom I managed to squeeze out a muted reply.

"Yeah fine thanks."

"Good. I was wondering if I could see you then?"

"Have you made an appointment?" A question I asked despite already knowing the answer, as I'd already seen the appointment book.

"No, I just thought I'd pop in and see you."

I struggled to hide my displeasure at seeing him (and the fact that I'd bought those three bars of chocolate needlessly).

"Well to be honest Mark you should have made an appointment. I could have been seeing another client. As it is I'm just about to go for lunch."

"So can I see you then?" he persevered.

"Go on then" I replied reluctantly.

I took him into my office.

I sat down.

He sat down.

Then he said something I'll never forget.

"I won't keep you long as I know you don't like me."

I was stunned.

I tried to regain my composure. I muttered some response along the lines of "don't be so ridiculous." But Mark had rumbled me. He'd sussed me out.

Bite Size Wisdom

Your attitude affects your behaviour and the way in which you communicate

From that day on things changed between me and Mark. I realized I had allowed my attitude towards him to move into the realms of complacency and indifference.

I had stopped being professional.

I had forgotten that I was being paid to serve Mark. Without any clients my services would not be required. It was because of people like Mark that I had work.

I had forgotten that.

I'd slipped into an attitude whereby I provided great service to the people I liked.

And because of my negative attitude towards Mark I found it rather easy to notice the things I didn't like about him.

So if I wanted to change my relationship with him I needed to change my attitude towards him. I started to look more for the positives. His work ethic. His willingness to take risks and start his own business.

And you know what?

It worked.

There was no moving reconciliation.

There were no tears.

But things got better between us. He became friendlier and less intense. We talked more about solutions to his business challenges rather than dwelling simply on the problems he faced.

Was it perfect? No. But it was better. He never challenged me about not liking him again, and I actually found seeing him a more enjoyable experience.

He hadn't changed particularly.

But my attitude towards him had. And as a result we developed a more successful professional relationship.

Bite Size Challenge

- So is your attitude towards someone hindering your relationship with them?
- Are you so blinded by the negatives you see in them that you're failing to see any positives?
- What's a small change in behaviour you can make to create a more positive (not perfect) relationship between you? Think of a specific thing you will do next time you interact with that person.

Be willing to be wr✗ng

W e like people who are decisive don't we? People who are clear on what they think and believe. People who don't dither or change their minds on a whim.

Focus, determination and confidence are all traits to be admired.

They're all signs of strength. They're traits I'm sure we all recognize every leader needs to possess in order to be a success.

And I agree totally with such a conclusion. But I also believe they could be the reasons for a person's downfall. They could be the reason why we don't succeed with people.

Let me explain.

Focus could lead to being blinkered in your approach. Determination could result in a stubbornness to change despite what the facts are telling us. Confidence could lead to a dangerous cocktail of arrogance and complacency.

It's probably fair to say that rarely at the top of a list of leaders' top traits would be "humility" and "a willingness to be wrong." A willingness to actually admit that in the light of fresh facts and new evidence a change of direction may be required. But such traits could be invaluable if we're to succeed in life and succeed with people.

When I'm driving and start going in the wrong direction (which happens on a regular basis despite the support of advanced modern technology) my sat-nav will advise me to make a U-turn. To ignore its advice, particularly when I'm in an unfamiliar area, would be stupidity.

Yet some political leaders, such as Britain's first female Prime Minister Margaret Thatcher, have baulked at such an approach. To make a U-turn was seen by her as a sign of political weakness. In some cases it probably was.

In some cases.

But ultimately an unwillingness on her part to ever admit she was wrong meant she lost the loyalty and respect of some of those closest to her, and this led to her unceremonious and premature departure as leader of her own party.

A similar stubbornness was fortunately demonstrated by Adolf Hitler. I say fortunately, because if he had been prepared to listen more to his generals and adopt a more flexible approach to Germany's war efforts then he may have tragically achieved the political outcome he was striving for.

Bite Size Wisdom

There may only be a subtle difference between "determination" and "stubbornness," but one leads to success whilst the other makes you look stupid

I'm not suggesting we abandon focus, determination and confidence. But I am suggesting this:

An overused strength can actually become a weakness.

However, this is not a call to embrace the complete opposite of these traits. But it is a challenge to be willing to temper them with a mixture of humility and openness when required.

Bite Size Challenge

How open and willing are you to having your ideas challenged by others? When was the last time you actively sought out someone to do so?

The reality is we need to be careful of becoming too black and white in our thinking about *every* issue.

Sometimes grey is OK.

Uncertainty goes with the territory in our ever changing world, and in order to embrace that uncertainty successfully, we have to be more open and flexible in our thinking and approach. That in a nutshell is often the key to succeeding with people.

OK, so what does this mean in practice?

It could mean not always trusting your gut feeling. Trust me; your gut feeling is not always right on every issue – particularly when you don't have all the facts to hand.

When you're meeting other people please remember first impressions are not always right either. They're powerful, and they're influential, but they're not always correct. But here's our challenge. We all have a propensity to jump to conclusions about people in our quest to pigeonhole them. We like putting people in boxes. It gives us a greater feeling of control. But this need to do so can have its downsides.

As you're about to discover.

Trusting my gut and going with "my first impression" has literally cost me thousands of pounds.

I've ended up working with people I should never have worked with. I've made important and significant decisions in my business and lived to regret them because I placed too much emphasis on my feelings and not enough on facts.

Once I'd made a decision I wasn't especially open to the possibility that I may be wrong. I persisted working with people I should have moved on from.

Big mistake.

To quote a proverb of the Dakota Indians:

"When you're riding a dead horse, dismount."

I'm not suggesting you ignore your feelings, but please be aware how much they can fluctuate.

So why not try this approach in future: Pre-empt your comments by saying "I may be wrong on this, but this is how I currently feel about things."

This encourages others to contribute their opinion without feeling they're attacking your position. It also gives you a get out of jail card which gives you the opportunity to change your opinion on a matter.

Clearly to do so all the time means you start to lose credibility, and in a time of real crisis this approach would do little to inspire confidence in others. But a willingness to be wrong and an openness to listen to and explore others' views and thoughts can be invaluable . . . sometimes. It's a great way to increase the engagement of others when you take such an approach and encourages others to share their own insights and ideas.

Fortunately a willingness to be wrong did contribute to the success of one of my bestselling books, *Self-Confidence*. That was the title my publisher came up with. I much preferred what I considered to be the far more quirky, engaging and sexy title *You Don't Have to Dance Naked*, with the subtitle *The real truth on how to develop your confidence*. Most of my friends agreed. In contrast the publisher's title was both boring and bland.

However I had to confess my publisher had a better understanding of the market than I did. They knew that the main book buyer of a well-known retailer in the UK would not support a book called *You Don't Have to Dance Naked*. It was just too quirky a title for them and the market they were aiming at.

But I had a gut feeling.

People would love the title. The word "naked" in the title would immediately arouse curiosity and interest.

But in the end I put my gut feelings to one side. I listened to my publisher. I went with their advice. I was willing to be wrong.

The question is, are you too?

So was my publisher right? Was my willingness to be wrong justified?

Well my book *Self-Confidence* was published in January 2010. It spent 24 weeks at number one in a particular UK retailer's business chart. It was quickly snapped up by a number of foreign publishers and is now available in several languages.

Who knows how well my alternative title would have done.

Even better perhaps? I doubt it.

My gut feeling was wrong.

It won't be all the time. And it would be stupid to ignore it. But it would also be stupid to make it the sole arbitrator of all my decisions.

Bite Size Wisdom

It's not a sign of weakness to admit you may be wrong; it's often a sign of wisdom

You need to weigh up your facts and not just your feelings. You need to listen to people who see the world differently to you. You won't always agree, but it would be unwise not to listen.

And when people feel they work for or live with someone who is prepared to listen to their perspective even when it may be different from their own, that can be highly motivating.

Agree?

Bite Size Challenge

Do you encourage people to challenge your thinking and viewpoint? Are you willing to admit you're wrong sometimes?

Don't
treat people as
(you) want to be
treated

It seems on the surface such a noble suggestion: treat people as you would want to be treated. And to be fair it's pretty good advice.

Up to a point.

Treating people with the degree of respect and courtesy that we would appreciate does seem a fairly reasonable starting place when dealing with others.

But please don't fall into the trap of thinking that what floats your boat also floats mine.

In fact, treating people as you want to be treated could have disastrous consequences and be the reason why you don't succeed with people.

Let me elaborate.

Kev is a key member of my team. He's quiet, intelligent, and also a little shy. Now, if you want to show your appreciation for something I have done then it's not stretching the point too much to say I can cope with some public recognition. And without trying to appear arrogant and conceited (which I realize I probably will) I quite enjoy being the centre of attention.

In fact, "enjoy" is not totally accurate.

I relish it.

Hey, that's how I am wired. I'm not expecting undying adoration and people throwing bouquets of flowers at me. Neither am I suggesting I want to be the sole focus of attention. But I'm comfortable with all eyes being focused on me. I'm a professional speaker after all. I thrive in such situations. I love making people laugh and meeting new people. It gives me a buzz.

Now let's go back to Kev. He sometimes accompanies me on my speaking engagements. If I wanted to show how much I valued him the last thing he would want is public recognition.

Call him up on stage and I doubt his legs would get him there. He would prefer the ground to swallow him up. He'd be embarrassed. It might well rank as one of his top ten awful moments on planet earth. His cry would be echoed in this next piece of wisdom:

Bite Size Wisdom

> Whatever you do, don't treat everyone the way you want to be treated

That's good to ponder isn't it? How often do we assume that what we'd appreciate others will too?

Well we'd be right.

Some of the time.

But there may be occasions when the opposite is the case.

I value Kev as part of my team, but I won't be organizing a big party in his honour and then inviting him up on stage to say a few words. I want him to remain a key player in the team, not resentful towards me for putting him through such an ordeal. (And Kev, if you are reading this, I promise I never will, OK?)

This insight has also proved invaluable in my relationship with my wife Helen. If I've received some bad news I like space. I need to be alone. I may go for a walk which gives me the opportunity to process my thoughts and come to terms with what I've heard.

After that I'm ready to talk to others.

Helen is different. When she's heard some bad news she wants to talk. If I gave her space and time to be on her own she might interpret that as not caring.

If I treat Helen as I would like to be treated I actually could cause a degree of pain and hurt. So although I walk, she prefers to talk. That's fine. We each respect that we both handle certain situations differently from each other, and over time we've learnt to respect that fact.

And this insight applies equally if you have children. It's certainly helped me in my relationship with my teenage daughter Ruth, who I talked about earlier. Helen, my son Matt and I are fairly tactile. We're comfortable hugging both privately and in public. Helen and I have been known to kiss occasionally, and even hold hands (although usually only when there's a full moon).

Ruth my teenage daughter is different.

Very different.

From an early age she made it very clear that "I don't like hugs and kisses."

Personally I didn't find that easy. I like to show my affection towards her. The only problem is, she doesn't like receiving it in the way I like to show it! But if I want to build a good relationship with my daughter then I need to treat her as she wants to be treated. Which means hugs and kisses are rarely on the menu.

However, Ruth has made it clear that expressions of affection in the form of buying her clothes, handbags and shoes are perfectly acceptable to her!

Now although the above may appear amusing, it has taken me time to adjust my expectations. However, I've learnt the following valuable lesson as a result of my relationship with Ruth:

Bite Size Wisdom

If you want to succeed with others focus on meeting their needs first rather than your own

Perhaps your relationship with someone has stalled because you've not taken time to consider what it is they see as important and what they would value. This applies equally at work as it does at home. Don't assume people value the same things as you. Our personalities are different, our interests could be, and perhaps more importantly so could what does and doesn't motivate us. Remember, what fits you might not fit them, so start treating people as *they* want to be treated.

And if you're not sure how people want to be treated, ask. Far better to ask than simply assume. So make sure you check out the following questions, as the answers could prove key to understanding how to develop more positive relationships both in and outside the workplace.

Bite Size Challenge

A great way to understand what motivates people and "floats their boat" is to ask these questions:

- In order for you to feel valued and appreciated by someone, what would they need to do to demonstrate that?
- What brings you most satisfaction from work?
- Describe a time when you felt particularly motivated at work.
- Is there one thing I could do to support you that I'm not currently doing?

Now over to you. Which of the questions do you need to ask to some of the key people in your life? When do you intend doing so?

Four killer
questions
you have to
ask **yourself**

Right, in this chapter it's over to you. The ball is being placed very firmly in your court. I'll serve the questions, but it's how you respond to them that will determine whether you move on to develop better and more effective strategies in how you deal with people.

While most books promise to give you the answers, I promise in this chapter I won't. But the answers *you* come up with could prove to be some of the most enlightening and insightful you'll gain from reading this book.

Here's the deal. In a moment I'm going to pose you four questions. Don't rush through them. And don't be intimidated either. This is not a test. There are no right and wrong answers. You don't even have to write your answers down or share them with anyone, although you might find it beneficial to do so.

This is simply between me and you.

To begin with I want you to think of a person with whom your relationship is of some importance. This could be someone connected to your work – for example; a colleague, your boss, a supplier, a customer. It's the kind of relationship where a breakdown or a problem between you would have consequences. So I'm not suggesting you bring to mind the woman you're on nodding terms with on the tube or train, or the guy you buy your sandwiches from at lunchtime.

Alternatively, the person you might want to think of as you go through the questions may have nothing to do with work. Perhaps it's a close friend, your partner (or ex-partner), a relative or even one of your children. It's probably not Aunt Kathy who you last saw 27 years ago, only keep in contact with at Christmas and have to think twice before you remember if she's even alive.

Get the picture?

Good.

Now with this person in mind reflect on these four questions:

1. What's going on in their world at the moment?

It's so easy to be wrapped up in our world and in our priorities that we fail to show sufficient interest in others. It's hard to connect with others and to build rapport when you have no idea about their world.

I'm not suggesting you do too much delving or ask them to lie down on a couch and ask them about their childhood. But I am asking you to take some time to reflect on this question. Perhaps it challenges you to stop and pause for a moment. Guess what? Not everyone is as fascinated about your work and your family as you are. Some people quite like to talk about themselves occasionally. Your answer to this question may possibly reveal some reasons as to why this person is behaving the way they are at the moment.

Now I appreciate some people are very private. They like to keep themselves to themselves. They wouldn't want to discuss what's going on in their lives. Fine. But that's not everyone. And if at this stage you realize your answer to this question is a little sketchy then perhaps that's an indication you should spend a little more time asking about them rather than simply talking about yourself.

2. What's important to them at this time?

Here are some possible things that might be important to people at the moment.

Maybe this person would really value some feedback on how they're doing at work at present. Maybe they just need some uninterrupted time with you. Perhaps they need a good listening to. Maybe they need some support or advice regarding a particular challenge they're facing at the moment.

Or it could be the complete opposite. Perhaps they just need some space and to be left alone at the moment. They could actually value you toning down your interest in them at times. (This is what I discovered with my teenage daughter, who doesn't want to talk much when she's with her friends and who frankly doesn't have a compelling need to answer my question "So what've you done today?")

Some people may not be performing to their usual high standards because they no longer feel valued or appreciated. Is it possible someone you know might be feeling a little taken for granted at the moment? Could even as little as 30 minutes' one to one conversation over a coffee make them feel far more valued? And could this change in how they feel lead to a change in how they act and behave?

Of course you could do some educated guessing around this question, or perhaps your relationship is such that you could ask the person directly.

For example, you could ask "If there is one thing that you'd value me knowing that would make our relationship even better or easier what would it be?"

It's your call, just make sure you do consider this question.

3. Am I listening to understand or listening to defend?

The author Dan Rockwell says "The road to excellence is paved with tough conversations." I think he's got a point.

The reality is that there are going to be times when in order to improve your relationship with others it will involve some potentially tricky and possibly difficult conversations. Let's not pretend these will be easy. They never are.

If someone is being quick to criticize you it's understandable that you'll be quick to defend. So the best way to perhaps de-escalate an issue is for you to simply shut up. Literally.

The other person could, as far as you're concerned, be speaking complete nonsense, but they still need to be heard. On the other hand, they may have a valid argument and provide an insight that you were unaware of.

Bite Size Wisdom

If you want problems to escalate make sure you hammer home why you're right and they're wrong. It works every time

The reality is that listening to understand rather than defend in these conversations won't be easy, but try lowering your defences, even just a little bit.

Perhaps you both have valid points. Perhaps there's just been a misunderstanding between you. So try listening to what the other person has to say rather than digging in your heels. Ask questions when you need clarification. And when you can agree with a point, say so.

Bite Size Wisdom

It's difficult to sustain anger with someone who's agreeing with you and trying to understand you

Here's an important point to remember though.

Listening to understand doesn't mean you'll always automatically agree with the other person's viewpoint. It simply means you're trying to understand their perspective. And when this happens they are then far more likely to listen to your point of view.

In my own relationship with my wife this particular question has proved both challenging and helpful. When Helen feels the need to give me . . .

how can I put this diplomatically . . .

"feedback"

my natural response is to listen whilst building up the case for the defence.

However, when I try to simply understand where she's coming from there have been numerous occasions when I've realized she has a valid point and I've needed to apologize. I'd like to say this is how we always resolve our differences, but the reality is that a combination of pride, emotions and fatigue mean we don't always adopt such an approach.

But when we do any potential conflict is invariably nipped in the bud.

Bite Size Challenge

How often do you consciously seek to understand someone else's viewpoint rather than automatically defend your own?

4. Have I clearly communicated my perspective?

The first three questions have been deliberately intended to help you focus on the other person's perspective and what's important to them. However, could the relationship between you both be helped by you clearly communicating your perspective?

Are you assuming that people know your priorities? Your agenda? Your needs?

Are you so clear in your own mind why a certain course of action needs to be taken that you've forgotten or overlooked the fact that others might not share your same clarity of vision?

Perhaps rather than simply telling people what needs to be done we need to spend a little more time explaining the "why." You might clearly see the reason why a certain action needs to be taken but others might not.

Bite Size Wisdom

> Don't expect people to "buy-in" before they've understood the "why-in"

Remember they might not currently have all the insights or facts on a situation you have. They might not appreciate the consequences of taking or not taking certain actions. And being told once about something is no guarantee they'll remember. Communicating your perspective may actually mean in practice reinforcing and reminding people of it. Regularly.

Here's a recap of the four questions:

1. What's going on in their world at the moment?

2. What's important to them at this time?

3. Am I listening to understand or listening to defend?

4. Have I clearly communicated my perspective?

Now having reflected on these questions, which were particularly useful to consider? All of them? Or one in particular?

OK, so what do you do with your answers and insights? Well that's up to you. I'm here to ask the questions. What you do or don't do with your answers is entirely your choice. But if I'm honest the exercise has been pointless if you fail to do anything as a result.

Agree?

Over to you then.

Bite Size Challenge

As a result of working through those four questions, what one specific action do you now need to take?

How to make criticism
count...
not
crucify

Have you ever received criticism or had to give feedback to anyone? It's not easy, is it? In fact people go on courses to learn how to give and receive feedback. I've delivered some myself.

One in particular springs to mind.

I was working just outside London, running a workshop on "Getting the best from people" and we were exploring the subject of giving feedback. This can be reasonably straightforward when what you have to say is generally positive, but can be as difficult as running through quicksand when it's not. Sensitivity, diplomacy, being balanced and constructive can all be required when the feedback you're giving could also be construed as criticism.

Let's not fool ourselves either into thinking that putting the word "constructive" before the word "criticism" makes it any easier for people to receive. It doesn't. No matter how self-assured an individual may be, they, like the rest of us, have a tendency to fast forward past the word "constructive" and to pause on the word "criticism."

Do we really care that the criticism will be constructive? Rarely. Ultimately, no matter how much you're going to try and package what you're about to say, it's still criticism. And when you use the word "criticism" it invariably triggers the raising of defences in most people (with the possible exception of politicians, who seem immune to it due to the excessive amount they receive).

That's why at my workshop I had been at pains to point out the pitfalls of using certain words when giving feedback. I recommend people to stay well clear of words such as "weaknesses" and bin altogether the phrase "constructive criticism."

So I have to say I was rather surprised by how Ian, one of the participants on my course, responded to a question.

I had asked the group to consider how they would approach someone whose performance they wanted to improve. I was encouraged by the responses of many of the group. Then it came to Ian's turn.

"Well I would tell my team member, Ben, that he has the potential not to be crap."

For a moment I thought Ian was joking. But I quickly realized he wasn't.

"Do you want to think of your use of language there Ian, and the impact of the words you use?" I asked.

"What, the word 'potential'?" replied Ian, with just a hint of sarcasm in his voice.

Now Ian might be an extreme example (and I really do hope he was joking), but how many of us have had our confidence knocked by what someone has said or written about us?

Bite Size Wisdom

Never underestimate the long-term effect of just a few brief words

Challenging people without undermining their confidence is not easy, particularly when you're having to do so with someone who is young and inexperienced. But there are of course those that go to the other end of the spectrum and sugar-coat their criticism to such an extent that the person hearing it thinks they've just been paid a compliment. Rather than challenge people about a piece of work or the way they're behaving we've ended up so wanting to avoid upsetting them that they feel they've just received a big cuddle, not a mild rebuke.

So is there a middle way? Is there a way of giving "constructive criticism" without actually having to use the phrase?

You'll be relieved to know there is.

Firstly, let's be clear in our own mind that our focus has to be on solving issues, not fixing blame.

Bite Size Wisdom

> We want our words
> to build up people,
> not beat up people

Here's a great strategy to do just that. I first came across this approach during my time working for the Chief Executive group Vistage (if you want to find out more about them please go to www.vistage.co.uk).

Like the best and most effective things in life, it's rather straightforward. Here goes.

When giving someone feedback, point out the positives by talking about *"what worked well"* and giving some specific examples. Point to any potential negatives or areas for improvement by beginning with the phrase *"even better if . . ."* and highlight how things can improve.

For example: "What worked well was the start of your presentation when you immediately engaged your audience by asking us a question." "Even better if you gave more thought to how you ended your presentation, perhaps by summarizing your main points and challenging us with one specific action."

It's almost disarmingly simple isn't it?

I've been using this approach for several years in my presentation coaching with clients, although it can be used in a number of different contexts. (I understand it's now an approach that's been adopted by some schools.) My goal is to be specific and clear in my feedback and having the above phrases helps me achieve this objective by focusing on what I'm going to say. If someone has several areas they need to improve that's fine. By using this approach the emphasis is on improvement, not criticism.

You can also ask people to reflect themselves on "what worked well" followed by "even better if . . .?" You're giving people a simple framework in which to focus their answers. Just remember though, not everyone has the necessary knowledge or awareness to answer these questions thoroughly or to everyone's satisfaction.

So the emphasis is primarily on you giving feedback rather than trying to tease out the information from someone.

Trust me; I've seen managers try the latter approach. It can be painful to watch. And time consuming.

Bite Size Wisdom

> We've sacrificed a lot in our quest to protect people's feelings by deluging them with diplomacy

I wonder if for everyone's sake we could just simply cut to the chase and get to the point. And that's exactly what we can do by using the "What worked well" and "Even better if . . ." approach.

When you do, remember the gloves are not off and be aware of the positive and negative impact of your words. Cutting to the chase is fine, telling someone they have the potential not to be crap isn't.

So after you've given your feedback you might also want to ask if they have any comments or questions about what you've said. Your points may need clarifying and if someone disagrees with your comments welcome this as an opportunity to discuss things further. You could end your feedback session by asking the person two further questions:

1. What have you learnt from this experience?

2. What, if anything, would you do differently next time?

Take the above approach with people and you've potentially motivated them to move on. You've made your criticism count, not crucify.

Bite Size Challenge

Identify a situation when you can use the phrases "What worked well" and "Even better if . . ."

There are of course some situations that arise where such an approach is not appropriate. Perhaps there's been a breach in health and safety or a major mistake has occurred at work leading to a loss in business or an extremely unhappy customer. Remember, even in such cases the emphasis is on fixing problems, not fixing the blame and destroying someone's confidence. To help you do so the following questions will help:

1. How did that happen?

2. Why did that happen?

3. What needs to be done now to resolve the issue?

Make sure you spend as much time on question three as you do on the first two. Avoid getting bogged down in the causes and make sure there's sufficient time given to solutions. This approach ensures people are motivated to improve and equipped to avoid a repeat of the same mistake.

Bite Size Challenge

Who in your organization needs support in how they give feedback to others?

Work out **why** they're

whinging

whinging

I wonder how much change you've faced recently, both in and outside work? It's hard to avoid really, isn't it? Apart from dying and paying taxes, it seems to be one of the great certainties of life.

It's a subject I speak a great deal about for organizations around the world. When a client who is experiencing significant change briefs me about their event, the context in many (but not all) cases is that there's a degree of negativity amongst staff and some resistance towards change. However, what surprises me is that some managers I speak to actually seem genuinely surprised by the amount of negativity emanating from their team in such circumstances, as if such a response is beyond the norm.

Well let's be clear.

Negativity is normal.

Sometimes it might even be necessary. An over optimistic approach to life can lead to self-delusion and not prepare us for the challenges that life will inevitably present us with.

So the real issue is not whether people are negative but what's caused them to be so and how long they'll stay in such a mindset.

You see I actually think negative people can get a hard time from others. Many motivational speakers and authors ridicule and mock negative people. They can become caricatured and perceived as being the root of all evil. Their attitude and behaviour is seen as firmly slamming on the brakes to progress and they can actually be treated with a certain amount of scorn and disdain.

I confess I've probably joined in such "neg bashing" in the past. I've worn my positivity with pride and looked upon the so-called unenlightened "neg heads" or "whingers" with a certain degree of patronizing sympathy.

I've felt justified in doing so. In many ways it can be quite good fun coming up with new labels to describe our negative friends and colleagues. Two of my favourites are "mood hoovers" and "B.M.W.s" – people who Bitch, Moan and Whinge. Such terms never fail to raise a smile from my audiences and colleagues. Using them is almost a guarantee of a cheap laugh. And such comments can be valid and describe very succinctly the behaviour of some people.

But I have my concerns.

Bite Size Wisdom

Giving people labels can be amusing, but they can also be limiting

Negative people and negative behaviour can be easily dismissed. Disregarded. Swept under the carpet.

But perhaps we're being too dismissive.

Perhaps there are genuine reasons for some people's concerns. For their negativity.

Rather than ostracize such people and ignore such behaviour we might well benefit from trying to understand what are the underlying reasons and causes for it. Rather than just respond to "what we see" a more effective approach might be to try and uncover and understand "what you don't see."

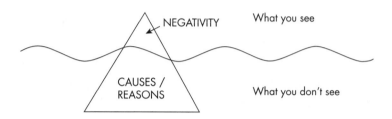

Let me be clear. I'm not suggesting that negativity should now be enthusiastically embraced and encouraged and we start each day thinking and discussing all we have to feel negative about. (You can watch the news if you want to do that.)

But I am saying let's be less dismissive of people's negativity and rather than see it as a trait that needs to be quashed immediately let's spend some time seeking to identify and understand why people are thinking and behaving in such a way.

There will be many reasons. Let's consider three to get us started.

1. Some people are miserable by nature

It's fair to say that some people you encounter in life wear their coat of negativity like it's an old long lost friend. It's comfortable. It seems to suit them. It's almost as if, if there is a God who's at the heart of creation, he or she has designated that a certain percentage of the population will have a negative or pessimistic outlook on life. Period.

Perhaps there's just very little some people can do to counteract their negative tendencies. Perhaps they've been wired this way to give the "positives" someone to poke fun at, or it's God's way of making sure there's some form of natural balance to the positive people.

Perhaps negative people's primary function on this planet is to assist positive people in keeping their feet on the ground and not getting too carried away with their ideas.

OK, I admit the above is written with a certain degree of tongue in cheek, but it does seem to be the case that some people's nature means they're wired to see the glass half empty.

Will they ever change?

Possibly not.

But they can learn to become more aware of how their negative outlook can impact them and those around them and learn to manage it.

They may never become naturally optimistic. Positivity will never be their default position, but you can help them to focus more on the positives and the possibilities and not solely focus on the negatives. (I developed seven questions to help you SUMO – Shut Up, Move On. They all would be relevant to someone caught up in the negativity mindset, particularly the final one: "What can I find that's positive in this situation?" To access the questions go to www.thesumoguy/downloads.aspx.)

Here's another possible reason for people's negativity.

2. A lack of self-confidence

People's negativity could in many ways be a misdiagnosed and slightly confused cry for help. Perhaps they don't feel very confident about themselves or a particular situation that they find themselves in, but rather than admit the fact (which to be fair might not always be easy to do) it is expressed in negative comments or a negative outlook. People may well look for reasons to justify their lack of confidence which in turn blinds them to the positives that also exist.

If a lack of confidence is someone's main reason for their negativity then some coaching, support and encouragement from someone else will be the required antidote and hopefully reveal that their negativity is more of a temporary condition rather than a permanent character trait.

This might not be the case simply in the workplace but, if you have children, also at home. A child's negative approach to a subject at school could be down to the fact that they don't believe they are very good at it and struggle as a result. Although some subjects may be perceived as simply boring, perhaps another reason for their negativity could be due to their lack of confidence. Some focused help in this area might not completely alleviate their negativity, but it might help.

Also be aware that for some people the lack of confidence that fuels their negativity stems from the fact they're doing something they don't enjoy or feel incapable of doing well. Remember, a fundamental human need is to feel confident in what we do.

Bite Size Wisdom

Teaching a pig to sing is not only hard work – its demoralizing for all concerned

So where possible, playing to people's strengths should see an uplift in confidence and in their attitude.

Here's a third possible reason.

3. A perceived sense of injustice

Sometimes people's negativity is simply a label bestowed upon them because they have failed to embrace a particular action or outlook. An unwillingness to do so is simply dismissed as a negative or resistant attitude.

Well part of that response may be due to a person's pessimistic nature or a possible cry for help, but equally it could be simply down to the fact that they don't agree with a decision or the reasons behind it. Rather than dismissing someone's negativity, which could further stiffen their resistance and deepen their resentment, at least try and appreciate where they're coming from.

Involve people in understanding the process in coming to a particular decision or outlook. Explain to them why this might not be an ideal solution but the reasons why under the circumstances this may be the most realistic way forward. Point out, if appropriate, the dangers of maintaining the status quo. Remaining there may feel comfortable in the short term, but could be dangerous in the long term.

Some decisions I appreciate are not open to debate and discussion. Quick decisive actions are on occasions the order of the day. But that doesn't have to be the case all the time.

Bite Size Wisdom

Rather than resent people's resistance, take time out to understand the reasons for it

Whilst it's unhealthy and unnecessary to analyze and justify every decision you make to people (although some organizations have been notorious for doing just that) the steamroller approach to communication is not our only other option. If you want to engage and win round people with a negative outlook, recognize their perspective could be valid. What they require from you above all is not necessarily a reversal of your decision and for you to automatically agree with them, but an acknowledgement and appreciation of where they're coming from.

Once you've done this it's likely that there'll be more cooperation and less time wasted on un-productive stand-offs.

Deep down most people want to be happy, not miserable. So your goal is to help people identify the reasons for their negativity and to help them through it. Look out for ideas in the next three chapters to help you do just that, whilst remembering the lessons from an earlier chapter – that some people are lightbulbs. They don't want to change, no matter how much you want to help them. Equally reflect on this point: Perhaps the main underlying reasons for a person's negativity are down to how they're managed.

Bite Size Challenge

Identify a person whose levels of negativity and pessimism seem above average to you. What do you think are the main reasons behind their negativity? What can you do to challenge or support them?

How to make people feel

S.P.E.C.I.A.L.

PART 1

I wonder if you've ever thought about the following: What's the real issue as to why people fall out with each other?

You see, behind all the gossip, the gory details and the fallout from our conflict with others lies a very important and often overlooked fact. The heart of the issue for many people was simply this:

"I didn't feel important."

People might not even be aware this is the reason and they're unlikely to articulate their feelings in such a clear way. But when you peel back the layers of frustration and hurt that often lead to anger you'll invariably find someone who doesn't feel valued or important.

It may have been triggered in many different ways: feeling ignored, lied to, ridiculed, overlooked, not listened to, not consulted, or being taken for granted. The reasons may be many but the impact is the same.

So in this chapter we're going to look at seven ways to ensure that people do feel valued and important. Because when they do they're going to be much easier to communicate and deal with. Applying these ideas will not only reduce the amount of conflict you experience but also increase the quality and depth of relationship you have with others, both in and outside the workplace.

To help us achieve such an outcome we're going to use the acronym S.P.E.C.I.A.L. to help us remember each of the seven points.

Here's what each letter stands for:

S erve

P ersonalized

E ncourage

C ourtesy

I nterest

A ppreciation

L isten

Now let's look at each point in detail.

1. Serve

An interesting word that for some people might conjure up associations more with a servant, or someone who works in a restaurant or retail outlet. It's probably not the first word on people's list of strategies to engage, influence and motivate others.

I'm suggesting it should be.

It should be something that becomes core to our character and at the heart of our attitude when we're dealing with others.

Having such an attitude of wanting to serve may have prevented my rather uncomfortable experience with Mark, whom we encountered in the earlier chapter "Check out your attitude."

You see, rather than believe that the world revolves solely around us and the only way to achieving happiness is to do all we can to get our goals met, we should in fact look at what we can do to meet the needs and goals of others. As the American motivational speaker Zig Ziglar says:

Bite Size Wisdom

"You can get anything you want in life, just as long as you help enough people get what they want"

As a professional speaker I regularly remind myself that my primary goal is to serve my audience. Of course I want to do a great job and be appreciated for what I do – I'd be lying if I said any different. But my main focus should not be

"What do people think of me?"

but rather

"What can I do to help meet my audience's needs?"

This automatically means I become more outward and less inward-focused. Ultimately my success comes from helping my audience. And a by-product of meeting their needs is that there's a good chance my own needs will be met too.

When an organization's main focus is how can we meet and ultimately exceed our customers' needs they're far more likely to be successful. When leaders ask "How can we best serve our staff to assist them in doing the best job possible?" they're putting service at the heart of their culture.

Now how you "serve" others specifically will depend on the person and the context. I'm not suggesting that after you've cooked a meal for a loved one you follow up with "Did everything meet with your expectations and what can we do to improve your experience next time?" followed by a questionnaire which on completion will be entered into a prize draw to win a free weekend in Whitby. Neither are you there to meet the every need of your children, although that probably will be the case at least in their first 18 months. (Notice I said months, not years.)

But you get my drift. Serving others is an attitude from which our behaviour flows.

So what does serving look like in practice? Well practical ways in which we can serve others will be revealed as we continue to look at how we can make others feel S.P.E.C.I.A.L.

2. Personalized

Go on, admit it, which would you prefer – a gift voucher or a present that has clearly been bought with you in mind? A valentine card with your name on it or one that says "To whom it may concern."

Get my point?

Make people feel special and important by personalizing your encounters with them.

In business you might well use customers' names when talking with them. I'm made to feel special when I'm working in a particular hotel I use regularly. They reserve a parking space for me with my name on it. Before I've even walked into the hotel I'm already feeling important.

My friend Mark Mitchell runs three car dealerships in the North West of England. He appears to have an obsession with doing all he and his hundred plus staff can do to make his customers feel special. Letters to customers often include a personalized note at the end from Mark. If he comes across an article that he thinks may be of interest to you he sends you a copy. It seems to be part of his DNA, but it's also good for business, judging by the loyalty of his customers.

In my own business when we send Christmas cards to our clients we personalize each one. Not simply by writing a personalized message inside, but by personalizing the cover of the card to include their name also.

There's no guarantee that if you make people feel special by making your encounters with them more personal they'll continue to do business with you. But you've certainly increased the chances.

With loved ones, rather than show your generosity with a cheque or voucher, perhaps a more personalized gift that required some thought on your part will have far greater impact.

Agree?

That's why the phrase "It's the thought that counts" is so true. Showing you've thought about someone even in only a small way can have a huge impact.

Bite Size Wisdom

> Treating someone in a way that is unique to them is a powerful way to make that person feel important

In terms of my own life, what does my wife appreciate – a diamond ring or a packet of midget gems? It's midget gems every time. Lots of men show their love by buying jewellery but my wife knows when I've bought her midget gems I've personalized my gift and given it some thought.

(OK, I've just shown my wife that last paragraph and she informs me that her ideal scenario would be a diamond inside a midget gem – but you know what I mean.)

Make it personal. Treat people as unique individuals with their own particular likes and dislikes and not just one of the crowd. And remember the point we made earlier in the chapter "Treat people as they want to be treated."

Bite Size Challenge

What one thing could you do this week for someone that actually demonstrates you've thought of them personally?

3. Encourage

I've been on this planet a long time. I've encountered hundreds of thousands of people on my travels, either meeting them personally or addressing them in an audience. To date I've travelled to 40 countries and spoken in 36. No one, but no one, has ever said the following:

"You know my problem? I've had too much encouragement."

Now admittedly, give me too much encouragement too often and it begins to lose its impact. But we all need encouragement sometimes.

My friend Lynda Stacey recently described herself as my CEO – Chief Encouragement Officer. We hardly see each other and rarely talk, but she still lives up to her title with her encouraging messages on Facebook or via text.

The word encourage literally means "to give courage." That might mean the courage to start something, the courage not to quit or the courage to aim higher. It could also mean that your encouragement gives people the confidence to stop something that clearly isn't working. But rather than feel a failure your words mean they've learnt from the experience and are better equipped for their next challenge.

Bite Size Wisdom

In a world of setbacks, disappointments and people who can be quick to criticize and pull you down, we all need encouraging sometimes

Your encouragement might be written on a card, a text, an email or a letter. It might simply be spoken. It doesn't even have to be long.

But words are powerful.

They have the ability to build up or bring down.

Throughout my life there have been countless people who've encouraged me. I remember how my friends Tom Palmer and Paul Sandham's comments had a profound impact on me on one particular occasion. Having seen my proposal for my SUMO book rejected by one of the top publishers in the UK their advice was simple: "Don't give up. Keep trying, at least for the next 12 months." Their words were exactly what I needed to hear, particularly after several setbacks. Within six weeks I'd signed a deal with a publisher.

There might not be any immediate tangible payback to you in encouraging others. There doesn't need to be.

But wouldn't it be great to look back on your legacy and realize that as a result of your words some people gained the courage to persevere or to aim higher? And the fact that you took the time to encourage them made them feel good enough about themselves to take the next step.

Well guess what?

You can.

Bite Size Challenge

Who in your world needs some encouragement? What can you do to make sure that happens?

How to make people feel S.P.E.C.I.A.L.

PART 2

So far we've looked at three ways to make people feel S.P.E.C.I.A.L. – Serve, Personalize and Encourage. Now let's look at four more ways. Remember, in doing so we're aiming to improve our chances of being able to influence, engage and motivate others whilst at the same time reducing the chances of conflict. Here's the fourth way.

4. Courtesy

The word "respect" is talked about a lot these days. There's even a political party in the UK that goes by that name. It's also a term that's become widespread in the sports arena, particularly within football. However, despite its increased usage I'm not sure if people even know exactly how to show respect to others.

Well here's a start. Show some courtesy.

Courtesy may seem an old fashioned word in today's modern society, but it lies at the heart of showing respect for others.

Never underestimate how positive the impact of using the words "please" and "thank you" can be on others. Or let me put it another way. Try being rude and discourteous to people and see how helpful and cooperative they become.

And courtesy shouldn't be used sparingly as if it's a rare and limited commodity or shown only to those you consider important. Neither should it be reserved solely for those who have in some way earned the right to be treated with respect.

Bite Size Wisdom

> Having respect for others should be our starting point in a relationship. Not a possible destination

Showing courtesy for others is a behaviour that is hopefully taught in schools, and needs to be modelled by parents and within the workplace. It's something I aim to do consistently with the people I lead in my SUMO team. You see, talking down to people and treating them rudely is another way of saying "you're not important, you're not my equal." Everyone, whatever their creed, colour, sexual orientation or history, deserves some courtesy and respect.

And courtesy is not just a simple case of saying "please" and "thank you." It's about thinking of other people's needs as well as your own. It's about replying to emails when you said you would. It's about returning someone's phone call like you promised to. It's about doing all you can to be on time for a meeting or event rather than drifting in when it suits you. It's also about choosing not to check out a text message during a conversation unless you've apologized for the need to do so.

Simple stuff?

Absolutely.

Obvious advice?

Probably.

And yet having been in business for over 20 years I still experience a lack of courtesy from people on an almost daily basis – fuelled in the main by a combination of ignorance and busyness.

But that's no excuse.

Bite Size Wisdom

> No one ever feels important when you keep checking your phone whilst they're still talking

Yet when we do show courtesy, even in only small ways, it all adds to the intangible mix of positive behaviours that develop our likeability. And when we're liked by others we're in a much better position to be able to influence them. People are more likely to be open to our ideas when they're open to us as people.

There are no guarantees of course, but you do increase your chances of engaging more effectively with others. Now I appreciate someone like Steve Jobs achieved outstanding success without always demonstrating this particular trait – in fact he had a reputation for being rude and discourteous with many people. And I realize there will be others like him. But I hope generally speaking such behaviour should be seen as the exception rather than the rule.

Agree?

Bite Size Challenge

- In what way may your behaviour be seen as discourteous to others?
- How courteous would your close friends and colleagues say you are?

5. Interest

Here's another obvious but often overlooked way in which to develop better relationships with the people you live and work with.

Be interested in people.

Stop obsessing about your own world and your own needs all the time. Show interest in what's going on in the world of other people.

Maybe just a simple question such as "Any plans for the weekend?" or if you're meeting for the first time, "Where's that accent from?"

Trust me. If you want to influence other people start by showing a *genuine* interest in them. But remember, if you're faking interest people will notice.

A sales assistant recently asked me if I had any plans for the rest of the day. I was pleasantly surprised by his interest and told him I was off later that day with my family to see the comedian Michael McIntyre.

His response?

Looking down at the items I'd just purchased he asked "Would you like a bag for those?"

My immediate thoughts?

"Hey pal, I wish you'd never shown any supposed interest in me in the first place. You've totally ruined the impact of your question by ignoring my answer. Rather than make me feel important you've now succeeded in hacking me off. And you've managed to do so in almost record time. Congratulations."

OK, maybe I was having a bad day, but you get my point don't you?

Bite Size Wisdom

> If you're going to ask a question, be prepared to listen to the answer

So if you want to connect with people remember to show some interest in their world and ideally don't just listen but also try and remember some salient points of what they've said. Even if it's just one or two headlines.

Why's that important?

Well what a great way to make an impression on someone next time you meet if you ask a question about something they talked about previously. So few people do this that you're bound to stand out from the crowd when you do.

Isn't this worth trying with at least one person you meet this week?

6. Appreciation

The author Philip Yancey states that the opposite of love is not hate – it's indifference.

I find that very challenging. Perhaps at times without even realizing it we can start to take our colleagues, customers or loved ones for granted. Complacency can creep up on us and if we're not careful our attitude towards others can slowly turn to indifference.

The antidote?

There are a number. Some of which we've explored previously, particularly in the chapter "No investment, no return."

Here's another.

Start showing that you do value the people around you and show some appreciation. Make appreciating others part of your core values and not an add-on to your to-do list if you get time.

Put some thought into it. Write a note. Send a text (although not when you're in the middle of a conversation with someone else). Make a call. Send a gift. Spring a surprise. Go the extra mile for a birthday or anniversary. How you do it is up to you, just make sure you do it.

You see, the very act of thinking about how you can show appreciation to others will in itself help arrest the advance of indifference.

With each of my clients I send a thank you card after I've worked with them. I never want to take their business for granted. I'm thankful for the opportunity they've given me. It's not a costly exercise and it takes minutes rather than hours to do. But it's now become a habit, and showing appreciation to others is not a bad habit to develop. And it's not just something to practise at work. It's equally important to show appreciation in your personal life.

My son Matt is training to be a doctor. Four years ago he wasn't sure what he wanted to do. Then his Biology teacher left and Mrs Shaw arrived as their replacement. She totally engaged Matt in the subject. So much so that that was the turning point in him deciding he wanted to be a doctor.

I wrote to Mrs Shaw to thank her for the impact she'd had on Matt. I told her she was M.A.D. – Making A Difference. In her reply she wrote "Thanks for letting me know. You made my year."

I hope showing Mrs Shaw some appreciation helps to continue to motivate her in her work, and reminded her of the positive influence she and other teachers can have on young people's lives.

Bite Size Challenge

Your mission for today, should you choose to accept it, is to show appreciation to someone in whatever creative way you choose. Feel free to share what you did and the impact it made by telling me about it. You can email me at Paul.McGee@theSUMOguy.com – I promise to personally acknowledge each email and you could get a mention in the next edition of the book.

7. Listen

Have you ever been talking to someone and it's become obvious they're no longer listening? How did that make you feel?

Now contrast that with the time when you really felt you were being listened to by someone.

It felt good didn't it?

Listening is perhaps a bigger subject than most of us are aware of. I simply want to put it back on your radar. Here's the reality:

Bite Size Wisdom

Sometimes being a person of influence is knowing when to stop talking and when to start listening

You see, I think we can be captivated by a great speaker, but we're often helped by a great listener.

But remember this. Listening is hard. If you think it's easy you're clearly not very good at it.

There are many challenges to doing it well. Thoughts pop into your head unannounced, sometimes triggered by what you've just heard. It's easy to be distracted.

Be aware that your prejudices inform your thinking, so it's difficult not to judge what you're hearing and be quick to offer your advice or opinion. Now that's fine in general conversation. It's to be expected. But it can also hinder you and become a barrier when all the other person wants is to be listened to.

And people rarcly tcll you the whole story. They miss stuff out. Leave gaps. If you don't listen well and don't ask questions you're not getting the whole picture. That can lead to problems.

To listen really well our attitude and starting point should be *"tell me more"* rather than *"here's what I think."* Remember, sometimes it's not about "us," it's about "them." If you want people to open up, to tell you more, to get to the heart of the issue you need to listen.

Develop "the gift of the gap." Yes, that's right, "gap," not "gab." Allow people space. Don't feel the need to fill every silence. Gaps in conversation are OK. They allow the other person time to clarify and articulate their thoughts.

If I'm angry, listen. If I'm upset, listen.

If I'm excited, listen. If I'm gutted, listen.

Sometimes I don't always want or need a solution. Sometimes I'm not after an opinion.

I just need to be heard. To be understood. To be listened to.

Bite Size Wisdom

Some people need to
tell you their story before
they're ready to hear
your solution

Perhaps then and only then do I feel ready to explore a way forward, and to listen to your perspective. You see, when I don't feel I've been listened to I'm less likely to be receptive to your thoughts and ideas. Your words wash over me.

Remember, I need to feel important. I need to feel understood. And perhaps the most effective way of helping to achieve both is to listen to me.

So will you?

Or will you just wait until it's your turn to talk?

Bite Size Challenge

Who do you know who needs a good listening to today?

So that's the final approach of how to make people feel S.P.E.C.I.A.L. Over the last two chapters we've explored seven ways to do that. Before we go on to our next chapter let's just remind ourselves of the seven again. As we do so which one in particular stands out for you? Serve, Personalized, Encourage, Courtesy, Interest, Appreciation and Listen.

How to pick people up when they're feeling down

Although it's unlikely that you and I have ever met I do feel fairly confident that I know something about your past.

My guess is that when you were a toddler learning to take your first steps, when you had the occasional tumble the people around you were not shouting:

"Loser – you'll never learn to walk."

Am I right? (And if I'm not I think I've just uncovered the main reason why you lack confidence, have low self-esteem and avoid taking risks in life.)

Sadly for many people all that encouragement they received when they were younger tends to disappear when they're older. But if we're to enable people to reach higher, to bounce back from setbacks and to achieve their potential, then we have to look for practical ways to help them, particularly if they've had a few falls recently.

So we're going to explore what you can do to positively influence and encourage people, particularly when for whatever reason they're feeling dejected, disappointed or demoralized.

Jesse Jackson said "Never look down on anybody, unless you're helping them up."

Wise words. But how can you do that?

Depending on the specific situation you will find some of the following help:

1. It's OK to not feel OK

Help people recognize that certain emotional responses to disappointments or setbacks are normal. To feel mad, bad or sad is OK. It's not wrong to feel that way. Actually, it's a sign that they care.

That's a good thing.

But there is a danger. People can stay "wallowing" in such emotions for too long. And that can lead to them making irrational judgements about themselves and others when emotionally low.

That's a dangerous thing.

So help people to understand that how they're feeling emotionally is normal, but also temporary. Like the sunshine in England it will be experienced from time to time, but it's never going to become a permanent feature of the weather landscape. Then help them to focus on the next points we're about to explore in order to help them move on.

2. Reframe failure

Let's be clear about what it means to fail. Firstly, failing isn't final. Neither does failing make someone a failure.

Just as falling is part of the process in learning how to walk, failing is part of the journey in learning, growing and succeeding. When people fail they're in effect receiving feedback. Maybe they need to adjust their approach, try a different strategy or practise more. It's not a permanent slight on their character.

Unfortunately, so much emotional baggage has become attached to the word "failure," that we need to remind people that anyone who has ever led a meaningful life has at some time failed.

So when people experience a setback acknowledge their disappointment and then help them to see it as helpful feedback for next time. It's part of their learning journey. It's not the end of it.

To help people do this use the two questions we explored earlier: "What can you learn from this?" and "What would you do differently next time?" By doing so you're helping people to focus on their future, not their failure.

Bite Size Wisdom

Failure isn't final until
you stop trying

3. Look for the positives

Setbacks and disappointments can grossly distort our perspective on reality. If you want to help people at such times remember to point out the positives. Be careful when and how you do this though, as it can sometimes be perceived as patronizing and possibly insensitive.

So I'm not suggesting if a friend has lost their legs in an accident that you march in breezily to their hospital ward whistling "Always look on the bright side of life" or state "Oh well, at least you've still got your arms." Depending on the situation tact and diplomacy may be required.

One of the most effective ways to focus on the positives is to question the other person to help them identify them.

Questions such as:

- "What did go well in your presentation?"
- "Which part of the exam did you feel you did well on?"
- "Think of a time when you did handle that situation well. What was happening then?"
- "What are the positives you can take from the experience? How can we build on them?"
- "What are some of the things that are going well in your life at the moment?"

Looking for positives when someone is feeling particularly low does not come naturally for many people. It's not a typical default response. Therefore people need to be both challenged and reminded in a supportive way that invariably it's not all bad news. However, make sure you do so without dismissing their pain or underestimating their disappointment.

4. Go for quick wins

How do you help people who are feeling demotivated? Simply remember the following:

Bite Size Wisdom

Nothing motivates
like success

As Thomas Carlyle said, "Nothing builds a sense of confidence and self-esteem like accomplishment."

So some form of success, no matter how small, can help fuel hope. That's crucial because it can breed confidence. It helps people to "move on" in a more motivated way, because people begin to believe they're capable of achieving success.

A great question to prevent people wallowing for too long is to ask "Right, what needs to happen now?" or "What's the one action we can take now that will indicate we're moving in the right direction?"

Make sure you make a note of those questions. They really will help you to help others.

When I talk about the importance of quick wins I'm speaking from experience.

Let me explain.

I'm probably best known for a book I wrote in 2005, *SUMO (Shut Up, Move On)*. However, what many people don't realize is it was rejected by 13 publishers (you may remember I referred to one of those rejections earlier). Each rejection came as a personal blow to my confidence. I actually received four negative replies on the same day. Boy was that a great morning!

But a quick win for me was to feel by the end of the day I'd taken some action towards getting my book published. That meant either tweaking my initial proposal (at one stage I actually considered dropping the phrase SUMO from the title) or contacting another publisher.

With one publisher who'd rejected my manuscript I still convinced them to meet me personally to discuss my book idea in more detail. They still rejected it, but the fact that they'd agreed to meet me felt like a small win. It fuelled my motivation and provided some momentum.

Now this next point is really important.

What I've discovered over time is that right feelings follow right actions.

By going for quick wins I am taking back some control and making some progress.

My motivation actually comes as a result of my action, not the other way round.

So in terms of helping ourselves and others to keep on keeping on, this next piece of wisdom is vital to remember.

Bite Size Wisdom

Focus on progress,
not perfection

It's not reaching the perfect score of 10 that counts to begin with. It's simply focusing on what actions are needed to help people get closer to 10. That means if someone is currently on "two" your aim is to help them to reach for three or four.

Yes, reaching "ten" may still seem far off but it's closer now than it was at the beginning of the process. So celebrate progress. Such an approach encourages people to persevere and not to become daunted by what they still need to achieve.

Remind people that success is ultimately an accumulation of small victories, and that's why achieving some quick wins can be vital in helping lift the spirits of people who are currently feeling demotivated or demoralized.

Bite Size Challenge

What quick wins could you identify to help your team or someone close to you come back from a setback?

5. Change location

Sometimes a change of environment or location can help stimulate a new perspective. A meeting in a pub or cafe rather than the office may help. Sometimes it might be going into the countryside rather than the city and on occasions maybe even a few days abroad.

Changing the physical space in which people operate has the potential to create a different outlook, generate new ideas and stimulate a new way of thinking by shaking up our normal routine and exposing us to a different environment.

A change can at times be literally as good as a rest and help provide the space necessary for people to rebuild, recover and re-charge.

Bite Size Challenge

We've explored five ways to pick people up when they're feeling down:

1. It's OK not to feel OK
2. Reframe failure
3. Look for the positives
4. Go for quick wins
5. Change location

Choose one strategy you can use to help someone when they've experienced a setback or disappointment.

How to **talk** so people **listen**

We can all talk. The problem is getting people to listen. Yet if we're going to successfully influence, engage and motivate those around us then it's important we understand what does and doesn't work when we're communicating with them.

Let's start by looking at three common communication mistakes that actually do more to switch people off rather than switch them on to our message. As we do, reflect on which ones you may have been guilty of or have seen others do.

1. Drowning people in detail

Almost everywhere I go I come across people who think the best way to convince and persuade people over a particular argument is to tell them everything they know on the subject. They mistakenly believe "If I bombard you with enough facts you're bound to submit to my way of thinking."

Wrong.

Bite Size Wisdom

People who are drowning in detail are usually gasping for insight

People are seeking clarity amidst the clutter of information being spewed out at them. But if they don't seem to be persuaded by what is being said, what do some people do?

Give you even more detail.

They press on regardless and ignore the tell-tale signs that they're losing their audience. People may be physically present in a conversation or meeting, but their mind is often somewhere else.

The biggest clue that this is happening is usually in their eyes. They glaze over. The lights are on but no one's at home. The wheel's turning but the hamster's dead.

Another perhaps less subtle clue that people have had enough of you talking is when they bang their head on a desk or do an impression of hanging themselves. Hey, even people with Self Awareness Deficiency Syndrome might pick up on these cues, although there's always someone who, despite your behaviour being strange, will press on regardless.

Bite Size Wisdom

Few people are bored into your way of thinking

The reality is most presentations and meetings would benefit by being reduced in time by 50%.

The harsh truth is that the applause some presenters receive at the end of their talk is not a sign of appreciation. It's an expression of relief.

It's also worth realizing that when you utter the words "to cut a long story short" most of your listeners are inwardly giving you a standing ovation.

So here's the deal. Brevity is best.

If people want more detail they'll generally ask for it. In fact you can always prompt them by saying, "That's an overview, does that cover what you need at the moment or would you like me to go into more detail about a particular area?"

In day to day communication perhaps in a more informal context the same principle still applies. Unless it's crucial for the other person to be aware of the full facts or it's a particularly exciting or humorous story then be content to just give the highlights, unless people ask for more. Even then make sure it's extended highlights and not a complete re-run of events.

2. Failing to make your message relevant to your audience

It's so easy to communicate content from your perspective alone. What may seem important to us may have very little relevance to someone else. But a failure to recognize this means you're wasting their time and your own.

Too many people start from the perspective "What do I want to say" rather than "What does my audience need to hear."

It's important we wake up to the fact that people will switch off unless your message is easy to understand, and most of all has some relevance to their own lives. Otherwise, what is the point of you talking?

3. Focusing on facts and forgetting the feelings

People aren't only interested and engaged by what you say but also by the way you say it. Appealing to people's intellect alone will rarely bring about change in them. You need to engage their emotions as well.

Bite Size Wisdom

When you want to persuade people, appeal to the heart, not just the head

So you'll need to give some attention to how you'll deliver your message and not concentrate solely on the content. That means thinking of ways to make your message more engaging and to consider what stories or anecdotes you can use to illustrate what you have to say. Remember Martin Luther King Junior didn't inspire a generation with the phrase "I have a strategic plan." He had a dream. He did focus on facts, but he also stirred people's feelings.

Too few people realize the importance of doing both.

Here's a recap of those mistakes:

1. Drowning people in detail.

2. Failing to make your message relevant to your audience.

3. Focusing on facts and forgetting the feelings.

Which ones have you experienced or perhaps been guilty of?

OK, so that's the problem. What's the solution? Well try these five ideas for starters.

1. Recognize their reality

Take time to think about other people's needs and concerns. Subconsciously many people, when you talk to them about a particular subject, are asking themselves "Why should I care?"

Think about where people might be struggling, or what problem your message might be the solution to. Tailor your message so that you scratch where people are itching. Because if you don't you'll have a polite audience but not one that's proactively engaged in wanting to hear what you have to say.

Prepare your content by keeping in mind that phrase in your audience's mind – "Why should I care?" And ask yourself "How can I make my message relevant to my audience?"

2. Remember the 90/90 rule

I can't prove this scientifically but potentially 90% of the impression you make on an audience has been achieved within the first 90 seconds of you communicating with them. And although all of your message will be important it's crucial that in those opening moments you grab people's attention.

Here are some examples of how you could do this.

- Start in a very clear and direct way:

  "I'm here to discuss the number one fear in most people's lives and how one simple idea can help you overcome it."

- You could start with a rhetorical question which by its very nature immediately engages your audience:

  "If you had to give someone just one piece of advice that you wish you'd received when you were younger what would it be?"

- Perhaps you start with a story or spell out very clearly in what way they will benefit from listening to what you have to say.

Just remember, inside 90 seconds you could already have people wishing they were somewhere else or engrossed and curious as to what you'll say next. So make sure you make those first 90 seconds count.

3. Begin with the end in mind

This point is actually the second habit from Dr Stephen Covey's book *7 Habits of Highly Effective People* (Simon and Schuster Ltd, 2004). It's a great approach to have and applies in life generally and to communication specifically.

It boils down to this. Are you totally clear on the purpose of your presentation, your meeting or your conversation?

To help you further, can you fill in the following blanks *before* you start your communication?

As a result of today's presentation/meeting/conversation the following will have been achieved:

Bite Size Wisdom

Take people on a clear journey. Not on a magical mystery tour

Remember, if you're not totally clear in your mind about the purpose and direction of your communication why on earth would you expect your audience to be?

Here's another great way to clarify things in your own mind.

Ask yourself what do you want people to know, feel and do after your presentation, meeting or conversation has finished?

Focus on these outcomes *before* you start preparing the detail, content and structure of what you're going to say.

Doing so cuts the clutter and provides clarity concerning what it is that is really important. The other additional benefit is that you'll save time. Both yours and your audience's.

Let me end this section with an example of a sign I saw on the centre of a table in the meeting room of one of my clients. It simply said this:

HOW IS THIS MEETING HELPING OUR CUSTOMERS?

What a great way of keeping people focused and clear on their ultimate purpose.

4. Point out the pain before providing the prescription

It's not easy for people to enthusiastically buy into a solution when they're not totally convinced there's a problem. In my presentations I often explore seven questions to help you SUMO (Shut Up, Move On). Here's a reminder of where you can access these: www.thesumoguy.com/downloads.aspx. They're particularly good questions to ask when faced with a challenge. The first one especially often resonates with people:

"Where is this issue on a scale of 1 – 10? (Where 10 = death)"

However, before I share these seven SUMO questions I first of all highlight the "pain" or problem of what I call "Faulty Thinking." This is a type of thinking that hinders both people's perspective and performance.

I tell stories and use examples to illustrate each type of faulty thinking and I ask my audience to discuss which ones they particularly relate to and do they also know people who "suffer" (I use that word deliberately) from these ways of thinking.

I then point out the impact and consequences when we stay stuck in faulty thinking and explain why being told "be positive" is not enough. I explain that people know they need to be positive, but when times are difficult and challenging they want to know how to do it.

What I'm doing with such an approach is taking my audience on a journey. I'm sharing anecdotes and stories with them, which is a powerful way to engage people at an emotional level. I'm making them very clear there is a problem when our thinking is faulty and highlighting the pain that can be caused as a result of that problem. You see, I don't just want people to understand the problem. I want them to feel it.

Do you think at this point they're keen to hear a solution?

You bet they are.

It's only then that I present the "prescription" to the pain, by exploring the seven questions. These help to provide a way for my audience to move out of "Faulty Thinking" and move on to what I call "Fruity Thinking," which is a positive and empowering way to deal with challenges.

Bite Size Wisdom

If you want people to buy into the solution make sure they've felt the pain of the problem

Remember, it's the combination of facts and feelings that causes people to engage with what you say and take action as a result. Don't focus only on communicating facts. Tap into people's feelings – and by pointing out the pain of a problem you do exactly that.

So is that something you could be more conscious of doing in future? You'll have to decide to what extent you point out the pain and how relevant and realistic such an approach would be within your particular context.

Perhaps worth a try though?

5. *Invest in yourself*

Learning to speak so people listen is easier said than done. Applying the ideas I've suggested and avoiding the mistakes I've outlined will definitely help. But if you're serious about developing your ability to engage and persuade your audience, whatever the size, then invest in some further training and coaching. Identify a coach you can work with or a course you can attend. Nothing beats the opportunity to practise and receive feedback to help your raise your game. If you're in the UK I'm happy to provide details of the services I provide in this area. Please email Paul.McGee@ theSUMOguy.com for more information. You can also check out a short video I made on the subject. Go to www. youtube.com/watch?v=mxQ-WWxP2w8

Alternatively check out the website www.TED.com. You'll have an opportunity to watch some of the world's leading experts speak on a variety of subjects. Learn not just from what they say, but also the way they say it.

Bite Size Challenge

So which of the following five strategies do you need to apply so that when you talk people listen?

1. Recognize their reality
2. Remember the 90/90 rule
3. Begin with the end in mind
4. Point out the pain before providing the prescription
5. Invest in yourself

Who else do you know who would benefit from discovering what's in this chapter? What action will you take to ensure they do?

The ball's in your court

So what impact can succeeding with people really have? Let's find out.

It was 10 January 1995. 4.30pm. I sat nervously waiting for Jacqueline's feedback. It had been an exhausting and challenging day.

Over the next two hours she unpacked in detail her thoughts on how the event I ran on her company's behalf had gone.

Those 120 minutes had a profound impact on me. As someone who had only three years earlier been battling the illness M.E. (or Chronic Fatigue Syndrome) I realized that in many ways it was an achievement even to be sitting where I was.

But I wanted more.

I wanted to develop my skills as a speaker and to grow my business. I wanted to achieve a dream not just to speak in the UK but also to audiences around the world.

As I sat listening to Jacqueline in the reception area of a hotel on the outskirts of Manchester I realized that what I was about to hear would either be the catalyst to fulfilling that dream or a wake-up call that I needed to dump my delusions and start thinking of a plan B.

September 1974. 8.45am. I walk into Mr Jeacock's classroom. I'm about to start my final year in primary school. My family have moved around a lot. It's my fourth different school. I'm ten years old.

My mum is passionate for me to succeed in life but academically I'm comfortably below average. Maths is confusing, science a complete mystery. I just wish I could quit education now and go to drama school. It's the only subject I seem to have any ability in.

Ten months later I leave school. I say goodbye to Mr Jeacock. I actually cry. I've loved those ten months. The happiest times I've ever had at school.

I've grown in confidence. Academically I've improved. Science is still a mystery to me though.

July 1986. South East London. It's the middle of the long university holidays. It's actually sunny in England. I've joined 50 or so other people to get involved as a volunteer in some community work for a Christian charity.

We're placed into teams with people who are strangers. Within days we're close friends.

My team leader is a guy called Paul. He's slightly older than me. We click. On the surface we seem to share few common interests though. He fails to understand the offside rule in football. I confess my love affair with Russian literature never even made it to a first date. But we laugh lots. We share a similar view of the world and have a deep fascination for people, and what makes them tick.

Twenty-six years later he's still my best mate. Where I'm at in life today has been largely influenced by him. On one level he's had no impact whatsoever in this book. He's yet to see a single chapter. But the wisdom, insight and experience that he's lavished upon me with a mixture of humour and amazing patience hopefully permeates many of the pages.

18 November 2012. It's Sunday morning. 6.30am. I'm awake early again. I've just binned the final chapter of this book.

Not a single word of it remains.

I've decided to write about Jacqueline, Mr Jeacock and my mate Paul instead.

They never needed to read this book. They were already living it.

They have already discovered how to succeed with people.

They're not perfect. They'll still make mistakes and have their challenges like all of us.

But I know the impact they've had on me. In their own different ways they've shaped who I've become.

Mr Jeacock instilled some belief and self-confidence into me. I was ten years old at the time. That's a good age to develop some confidence.

Jacqueline's professionalism and encouragement meant her feedback of my first speaking event in January 1995 did not crucify me. It became a catalyst for my career.

And Paul's ongoing support, despite some of his own personal struggles, means I've had the privilege of having a mentor and role model as well as a mate.

Between them they've shown me the impact succeeding with people can actually have.

It really isn't pink and fluffy stuff. It can be life enhancing. More than that, applying even only a few of the ideas we've explored in this book can be life changing both in our personal and professional lives.

But whether they are or not is down to you.

Your challenge and mine is not acquiring more knowledge. It's not even about coming up with new ideas. It's about doing something with what we know.

It's about realizing that all we've explored so far is easy to do.

It's also easy not to do.

So will this book just be another one to put back on the shelf and leave undisturbed for the next few years? Will some of the ideas and insights you've gained be quickly forgotten?

I hope not.

In fact, I hope you challenge yourself to do something right now. I'm putting the ball in your court and asking you to do something that will probably take less than five minutes.

Contact me. Tweet your feedback of the book to @thesumoguy, or email me at Paul.McGee@theSUMOguy. com.

All you have to do is tell me one thing that has stood out for you from this book. Then tell me one thing you're going to do as a result of reading it.

You're probably thinking you can't be bothered.

You're probably thinking it doesn't really matter.

You'd be wrong.

It does matter.

I personally read all the feedback I receive. And I reply. But you're doing this for you, not for me. Taking just one small action can prove the catalyst to taking further small actions. It's a quick win and we already know how good those can be for us, right?

Whatever our future contact, I really do hope that in some small way this book has been of help. Life can be quite a rollercoaster at times, particularly when it comes to dealing with people. They can be our greatest source of joy and our greatest source of heartache.

Mr Jeacock is no longer around to read about his legacy to me. Paul and Jacqueline are.

I hope that having shared this journey with me you now feel equipped and inspired to leave your own legacy in people's lives.

The great thing is you can.

You can actually start today if you want to.

The ball's in your court.

One final thing before I go. Here's a brief reminder of some of what we've covered.

I hope it helps.

How to succeed with people

People can't be fixed. Helped and supported yes, but not fixed. We're not machines. Always remember that.

Most people suffer from S.A.D.S. – Self Awareness Deficiency Syndrome. If you think you've not got it you probably have. So be open to feedback. It could be a real gift to you.

Some people won't change. They don't want to. They're lightbulbs. Unless you find the right switch. That's reality.

Intelligent people do stupid things. A high IQ does not mean automatic success with people. They don't give out degrees in common sense. So be humble.

Remember, you get what you tolerate. Your silence speaks. But not always the message you want. So speak up sometimes.

Humiliation is for amateurs. It's a sign of weakness, not power. Get help if you need to. And take humiliation for a very very long hike.

Being nice won't always work. Sorry to be a pain, but it won't. But being unpopular may be the right way to be. Sometimes. And that shows strength.

Remember, one person can make a difference, but it takes two to tango. Have the courage to ask yourself if you're contributing to the problem. That's brave. It's also incredibly helpful.

If you're not making the investments don't expect a return. Money doesn't grow on trees and relationships don't survive on indifference. That's the deal until you start making some deposits.

Set your expectations high, but make them realistic. That's unless you're addicted to stress. And that's not OK.

Let sleeping dogs lie sometimes. But make that an option, not a lifelong strategy. OK?

Check out your attitude. It's more important than you'll ever realize, and could rescue a relationship. Just ask Mark.

Hang up your need to always be right. You delude yourself when you believe you always are. You're not. So be willing to be wrong and then see how much real success you achieve.

Treat people as they want to be treated. You'd be surprised how much you gain when you first help people get what they want. Treating everyone the same is naïve. So be flexible if you want to be successful.

When you know what's going on in people's world and what's important to them you're building a better relationship. When you listen to understand and communicate your perspective you're on the way to building a brilliant one. That's to be desired.

When you talk about *what worked well* and *ever better if* . . . you're making your words count, not crucify. That can resurrect people's confidence and redeem a relationship. That's powerful.

When you work out why they're whinging you'll realize there are often reasons for people's resistance. They need to be listened to, not labelled. That's respect.

People need to feel S.P.E.C.I.A.L. because we're all important. And when you meet that need you really do help people succeed. That's a privilege.

When people feel down you can help them up. You may need to reframe failure, go for quick wins and allow them time to feel down. For a while. But that's just one chapter of the story. You can help them write a new one. That's exciting.

And make sure you're heard. Talk so people listen. You've got a message to bring. Don't lose it in the detail. Bring it alive with facts but don't forget the feelings. Engage, influence and motivate.

That's how you succeed with people.

About Paul McGee

Told at school "you'll never get anywhere in life talking all day," Paul McGee is one of the UK's leading speakers on the areas of change, confidence, workplace relationships, motivation and stress. His thought-provoking, humorous and practical approach to life's challenges has seen him speak in 36 countries to date and he is the author of nine books. He is also a performance and life coach working with one of the English Premiership's leading football clubs.

The proud creator of S.U.M.O. (Shut Up, Move On), his simple yet profound messages have spread across the globe both in public and private sector organizations. More recently his ideas have been developed for young people under the banner of SUMO4Schools.

Building on his academic background in behavioural and social psychology, Paul is also a trained counsellor, a performance coach and a Fellow of the Professional Speaking Association.

His aim is simple – "I want to help people achieve better results in life and have more fun in the process."

For more information visit **www.TheSumoGuy.com** or follow Paul on Twitter: **@TheSumoGuy**

More stuff to help

To build on the ideas and insights gained from this book you will also find the following helpful:

- *The Snowball Effect: How to Make Your Communication Unstoppable*, Andy Bounds (Capstone).

- *How to Win Friends and Influence People*, Dale Carnegie (Vermilion).

- *The 5 Languages of Appreciation in the Workplace*, Gary Chapman and Paul White (Moody).

- *Influence: The Psychology of Persuasion*, Robert B. Cialdini (Harper Business).

- *Switch: How to Change Things when Change is Hard*, Chip and Dan Heath (Random House Business Books).

- *How to Persuade and Influence People: Powerful Techniques to Get Your Own Way More Often*, Philip Hesketh (Capstone).

- *Fierce Conversations*, Susan Scott (Piatkus Books).

Other titles from Paul McGee

Self-Confidence: The Remarkable Truth of How a Small Change Can Make a Big Difference, 2nd edn, Capstone Publishing, 2012.

S.U.M.O. Shut Up, Move On: The Stright Talking Guide to Creating and Enjoying a Brilliant Life, 2nd edn, Capstone Publishing, 2011.

S.U.M.O. Your Relationships: How to Handle Not Strangle the People You Live and Work With, Capstone Publishing, 2007.

How to Write a CV that Really Works, How to Books, 2009.

Bring Paul McGee to your organization

Paul McGee speaks around the world at team events, conferences, workshops and retreats. From a one hour keynote presentation to a three-day seminar, Paul can tailor his material to your specific requirements, primarily in the areas of:

* Succeeding through change

* Managing, motivating and leading people

* Building winning relationships with customers and colleagues

* Maximizing your potential, maximizing your performance

* Surviving and thriving under pressure

* High-impact presentation and communication skills

As one client said, "I saw Paul present at a conference in Mauritius. He uniquely addresses one of the biggest barriers to personal and business development . . . our own minds. The SUMO philosophy was a unanimous hit. Very,

very powerful stuff!" **Simon Newton-Smith,** *General Manager, Virgin Atlantic, Southern Africa*

In order to make contact with Paul or learn more about SUMO4Schools

Email **Paul.McGee@theSUMOGuy.com**

visit **www.theSUMOguy.com**

or telephone **+44(0) 1925 268708**

Follow Paul on Twitter: **@TheSumoGuy**

Index